ENCOUNTER

with

HELL

About the Author

Alexis McQuillan (Pacific Northwest) is a paranormal consultant, researcher, and author. She's been actively involved in the paranormal community for over twenty years.

MY TERRIFYING CLASH WITH A DEMONIC ENTITY

ENCOUNTER

with

HELL

ALEXIS MCQUILLAN

Llewellyn Publications
Woodbury, Minnesota

FIRST EDITION
First Printing, 2012

Cover art: Spooky elements: iStockphoto.com/stereohype
          Dirty edges: iStockphoto.com/cajoer
          Demon: hektor2/Shutterstock.com
Cover design by Adrienne Zimiga
Edited by Patti Frazee

Llewellyn Publications is a registered trademark of Llewellyn Worldwide Ltd.

Library of Congress Cataloging-in-Publication Data

McQuillan, Alexis, 1957–
  Encounter with hell : my terrifying clash with a demonic entity /
Alexis McQuillan. — 1st ed.
      p.   cm.
  Includes bibliographical references.
  ISBN 978-0-7387-3350-0
  1. McQuillan, Alexis, 1957– 2. Parapsychology—Biography. 3. Ghosts.
  4. Demonology. 5. Spiritual warfare. I. Title.
  BF1027.M37A3 2012
  133.4'2092—dc23
  [B]
                                                          2012019127

Llewellyn Worldwide Ltd. does not participate in, endorse, or have any authority or responsibility concerning private business transactions between our authors and the public.
  All mail addressed to the author is forwarded but, the publisher cannot, unless specifically instructed by the author, give out an address or phone number.
  Any Internet references contained in this work are current at publication time, but the publisher cannot guarantee that a specific location will continue to be maintained. Please refer to the publisher's website for links to authors' websites and other sources.

Llewellyn Publications
A Division of Llewellyn Worldwide Ltd.
2143 Wooddale Drive
Woodbury, MN 55125-2989
www.llewellyn.com

Printed in the United States of America

Contents

PROLOGUE

There comes a time in some ghost hunters' lives when the tables get turned and the hunter becomes the hunted. It doesn't happen to all ghost hunters, but it does happen. It especially happens when the hunter goes out of his or her way to go to the places that the other hunters won't.

You know the places: they're the places that people only whisper about in the dark corners of bars or in out-of-the-way booths at the backs of restaurants—the places that aren't talked about in polite company.

Almost every city has one. It could be the old deserted house down the street, the lonely dirt road out in the country, or the cemetery everyone passes by a little faster when they're out walking or in their cars. It's the place you warn your kids to stay away from or your parents warned you to never even think of going to, even out of curiosity.

The place could be the subject of an urban legend that has been around for years. Even urban legends have a grain of truth to them—most of the time. It's the urban legends that sneak up on you and get you, especially when you're not expecting it.

It starts out innocently enough and turns into something so ugly and vile so quickly that by the time you realize what's happened, it's too late. You find yourself caught up in a web of evil with no way out. Even when you think you've escaped, you really haven't. You just lie to yourself to make yourself feel better and to make it through another day, week, or year.

But deep down inside you know you'll never escape; there's no place on earth to hide because it will find you again—anytime it wants. You bury the thoughts lingering in the hidden recesses of your mind that tell you there's no longer any place for you that's truly safe. In your darker moments you even wonder if you will be safe in death.

Sound like a horror movie? It's not. It's my life. And the creature that haunted my life is not alive; well, not in the normal sense of the word. The beast is a demon. You don't believe in demons? That's okay. I didn't believe in them either, which is how I got into this mess in the first place. I should probably qualify that statement. I've always believed in dark or negative spirits. To me, demons seemed like a fabrication of the Church, used to keep their subjects in line. But to say demons actually existed….yeah, I wasn't ready to take that step.

I got involved with ghost hunting when I was in college and, between getting married and raising children, I've continued to ghost hunt for the last twenty-some years.

At first my family thought I was nuts to go roaming around cemeteries and abandoned buildings in the middle of the night. Now they've come to accept that my world is a little weird and I'm not a typical mom. I'm also convinced my neighbors think I'm a cat burglar because I dress all in black and carry things to and from my car in the middle of the night.

The truth is, I'm what some people call a "spirit walker," others call a "sensitive," and still others call a "medium." Personally, I'm not very fond of the word "medium" because of how Hollywood and other media has portrayed mediums, but you can't run from what you are. In other words, I see and communicate with dead people, which, as I'm sure you can surmise, leads to some rather amusing situations. However, it also leads to a lot of things that aren't so amusing, which you'll find out as you read this book.

I've been able to see and talk to the dead as long as I can remember. Communicating with a ghost can be a unique experience. Sometimes they show me pictures or movies in my head using telepathy, but other times I see the events they show me play out in front of me, like I'm watching a play or television. At other times, they just speak telepathically to communicate a message.

When I reached my late 30s, after my children were grown and out on their own, I began to take a larger interest in developing my gifts and started to read about working with energy. It seemed logical because ghosts, spirits, and everything around us is made up of energy, and I can feel the energy of a place or ghost without any trouble.

Because of how ghosts communicate with me, I came to the conclusion that I'm not psychic; my brain just interprets energy differently and can turn that energy into pictures, showing me a snapshot of the past events of a location or person.

Experimentation led me to discover that I can use my own energy to manipulate other energies in various ways. For example, if a ghost gets too close I can use my energy to push them back. Think of it as a force field that can be expanded or contracted at will.

I also feel it's important and relevant to the story you're about to read to tell you about an event that happened to me when I was fifteen.

I awoke out of a sound sleep and felt like I was being attacked by something. I couldn't see anything, but I could feel it. It felt heavy, evil, and hateful. I felt like I was fighting for my very soul. To this day, I'm convinced that was the case.

Not knowing what else to do, I started to recite the Lord's Prayer, asking God for help. I was desperate and scared to death. I mean, I've always seen g hosts, but never had any of them attack me.

Within seconds of me saying the prayer and calling for help, my entire bedroom filled with an amazing white light. It was brilliant, but didn't hurt my eyes to look at it.

At that very moment, whatever was attacking me left in a hurry. I sat up in bed, gasping for breath, and still staring at the light that filled my room. It seemed to be just about everywhere, but didn't appear to come from one main source.

A minute or so later the light condensed into a smaller form and started coming towards my bed. Instinctively, I knew there was nothing to fear so I sat perfectly still, scarcely daring to breathe.

The light began to wrap around me like a blanket, and I can't even begin to adequately describe the feelings of warmth, peace, safety, and unconditional love that filled my soul. I mean, I could physically feel my body filling up with these emotions.

My entire body luxuriated and relaxed in the warmth and safety of this white light, and I was thankful that, for some reason, help arrived when I needed it most. The light slowly faded away, and I lay back on the bed. I swear I heard a voice tell me to go back to sleep, that angels would be watching over me and I had nothing to fear.

I knew in that very instant that God did exist and he did protect and watch out for people; that maybe I wasn't supposed to see him like other spirits and maybe you needed unwavering faith and belief in order to "see" him.

Either way, God saved me that night, and to this day, I still don't know why. If I was worthy of him saving me, there must be a reason, a purpose to my life that I'm still not sure I fully understand.

This event gave me a newfound courage and the strength to deal with just about anything that came my way throughout my life—including the demon. To me, there is a big difference between believing in God and knowing there's a God that watches out for people and protects them.

Because I'm not a big believer in organized religions, I studied many religions including Paganism and Wicca.

Paganism is an earth-based religion where followers believe in more than one god and goddess. Most practitioners of Paganism choose one god or goddess they connect with for their main deity.

Wicca is a religion that involves the ritual use of magic that is usually drawn from previous centuries. Wiccans typically believe in a god and goddess and have a very high moral code called the Wiccan Rede. One of the main moral codes of those that practice Wicca is "an it harm none, do what ye will." In simpler terms, "first harm none."

I draw from many belief systems to find what works for me and discard the rest. I took a particular liking to candle magic and studied it extensively for several years. Personally, I think it's my eclectic belief system that helped save me from the demon. I wasn't bound by one set of religious beliefs, so I could use what I learned from many different ones to make myself stronger. I also believe that my unwavering faith in God gave me the courage to combat the evil that invaded my life.

It's taken me ten years to set this tale to paper. Even the thought fills me with a deep sense of dread, yet a sense of excitement at the same time. I have no clue what the demon will do, how he will react, or who's going to pay the price this time.

The thought of reliving that time is really hard for me to even wrap my head around. When I think back to what he did, how he did it, and how completely stupid I was not to even see it until it was almost too late is beyond me.

I honestly can't believe I'm still giving that vile beast this much power after all this time. But that's what demons do, you know? They crawl into your head and take up residence; they screw with your mind, your sanity, your emotions. Even when you think you're rid of them, you're really not.

Demons mark your very soul, the essence of who you are, or were, whatever the case may be. They leave you shattered, worn, shaken, and beaten down, exhausted and emotionally and psychologically fragile. Yet you have to keep fighting. There's no other choice. It's spiritual warfare at its highest level. Good versus evil, light versus dark.

It's for the very reasons stated above that I haven't told my children or husband about the demon. To me, it's the only way I can keep them safe—keep them away from the darkness and evil that I walked through and continue to walk through to this day.

My children have the same abilities I do; they just have chosen not to use their gifts, which is probably for the best. A demon is capable of easily destroying a gifted person who is not trained in the use of their gifts. My husband still doubts my gifts and abilities, along with the existence of the paranormal. In some ways that's good. It keeps him safe. I can keep him at arm's length and not have to explain a lot of things I'm not sure I could explain. Yet it's hard for me sometimes to not be able to share the things I see and experience. Over the years, it's put somewhat of a wedge between us. Now that I look back on my experiences with the demon, that's not exactly a bad thing. His not believing is what is keeping him safe—and that's all that matters to me.

One of last times I came in contact with Amon the demon was when I went to the cemetery just down the road from the house Amon lived in. I'd stopped to visit the graves of the original owners of the house who died in the 1800s.

When I arrived at the gravesite, I got out of my car and went to pay my respects. The air around me grew very still and silent, and I could feel the approach of some type of phantom, but it wasn't close enough for me to distinguish its energy.

I turned around in the direction of the energy and, within a couple of seconds, felt the demon's presence about a hundred feet away and closing in fast.

"Amon, you must leave me be. There is no place in my life for you or any of your kind," I said calmly, putting my hand out in front of me to use my energy to stop his.

The demon's energy stopped advancing towards me, but the wind picked up and with it came blistering cold air. I knew it wasn't the weather—it was sixty-five degrees and sunny outside.

I started to shiver in the demon's presence but refused to back down or flee from the beast's energy. I dropped any protective shields I'd had around me in order to let my gift of sight take over and show me exactly where Amon was standing.

Within a few seconds I could "see" the demon standing by a large tombstone about fifty feet away from me. His bright red eyes, deeply set into his massive wolflike head, bored into me, sending shivers of fear down my spine I quickly buried. The foul stench of rotten eggs, quite common in the presence of such a beast, reached my nostrils as the scent rode the wind towards me.

Every fiber of my being was screaming at me to race to my truck and get the hell out of there, but I fought against it. To flee now would be perceived as a sign of weakness by the mighty demon, and weakness is the one thing you should never show to a demon or any other type of dark entity.

"If you have something to say, now would be your chance." I said, sounding a lot braver than I felt.

Telepathically, I could hear Amon. He said, "I know you want to run. I can feel you trying to hide the fear you feel being in my presence. You and I aren't that different, you know. We both wander this earth in search of something. You may be a child of the light, and I of darkness, but in the end, we shall see which prevails. Remember, I can haunt you all the days of your life."

With those words I felt Amon's energy begin to dissipate and the coldness that enveloped me turn to warmth. I walked slowly back to my truck, thinking about the words the demon had spoken. I'm still not exactly sure what he meant, or whether it was a veiled warning, but only time will tell.

The events described in this book are true. They are evil, vile, and terrifying events that have left a stain on my soul, a mark on my very essence. I know I have nowhere to run, no way to escape, and there is no safe place for me any longer.

But truth be told, I'm tired of living in the shadows, hiding in the mists, and always looking over my shoulder, being ever vigilant—walking between two worlds, so to speak.

It's time to begin my tale, but I leave you with one final warning. Be careful. If you're religious, cling to your faith with every fiber of your being. I say this not scare you, but to try to protect you. I know what this thing can do. Soon you will too.

As a final note, the location and names have been changed to protect the innocent—if any can be found.

Alexis McQuillan

CHAPTER ONE

Before I begin the story, I thought it best if you familiarized yourself with how demons behave, what they do, and how they do it. As you read my tale, the information in this chapter will help you put the story into context and help you understand just how sneaky and insidious demons really are.

CHARACTERISTICS OF A DEMON

First, I am not a demonologist. I can only speak to the demon that invaded my life and what information I've been able to gather from doing some research about demons— and what I believe in my soul. The demon I happened across is named Amon, a powerful demon in the anarchy of the demon world.

In the Ars Goetia, which is the first part of the Lesser Key of Solomon, Amon is listed as the seventh most powerful demon. The word *Goetia* refers to the type of magic that allows the person performing the spell to call forth demons and angels.

People who practice Goetic magic believe that by calling forth demons they can then become immune to the demon's temptations and banish them from their lives, therefore bringing them closer to God.

I've talked to members of clergy and conducted some independent research and my conclusions follow.

I'm sure there are demonologists out there who will disagree with what I relate to you in this book, and I'm good with that. My only comment to them would be: How many of you have actually encountered a demon?

Many demonologists believe that demons have specific, different characteristics than spirits. For example, because demons have never been in human form, or alive in the sense you and I are, some people believe that demons are jealous or resent the living.

Another common characteristic demons have is that, while they certainly have the ability to physically harm the living by scratching, biting, causing welts, pushing or shoving people, etc., they seem to prefer to attack the human mind by causing extremely oppressive fear and anxiety.

Many demons make their presence known by growling or emitting an odor that resembles rotting eggs or decaying flesh. I can tell you from firsthand experience, it is a very distinctive scent unlike any other and, once you've smelled it, you'll never forget it and could recognize it anywhere in a heartbeat.

While demonologists, religious leaders, and paranormal researchers may argue certain aspects of demons and their behavior, and how they came into existence, there is one thing most can agree on: somewhere out there are hateful, evil, resentful, and terrifying creatures that can make their way into our world to hunt down and torment the living.

I feel it's important, as you read my story, for you to understand how this particular demon wormed its way into my life before I even knew what had happened. But remember, I didn't believe in demons at the time these events took place.

If I'm being brutally honest with myself and with you, dear reader, the truth is that Amon worked his way into my life because I let him—not consciously, of course, but the fact remains that most of what happened to me was my own fault.

I'm the one who kept going back to the Matthews house where Amon lived. I'm the one who kept seeking the demon out in an effort to learn more about how Amon thought, behaved, and reacted to certain things. I became fascinated and obsessed with this demon; whether he played a part in that behavior, I don't know, although it's possible. However, whether he did or not really doesn't matter. I'm the one who made the choice to keep going back to that house when I could have stopped myself anytime I wanted.

The Arrival of a Demon

One of the main questions I never found an answer for is how Amon ended up living in the Matthews house in the first place. My research has shown there are many ways to summon a demon, even if that's not the intent. Some people believe that a demon can just show up and invade your life.

Personally, I believe that a demon needs to be summoned and/or invited in order to invade a particular place. There are many ways this could occur.

For example, a Ouija board in the hands of someone who has no idea how to use it properly could invite a demon into a person's life. The basic theory behind a Ouija board is that it opens a door to the other side and anything—good or evil—can choose to walk through that door. In other words, it's like an open door to your house.

If you insist upon using a Ouija board, say a prayer of protection before you begin your session, and light a couple of white, previously unused candles. For example, you can say: "God (or whatever supreme being you believe in), please protect us from any evil that tries to invade this space and keep us safe from harm. Amen." You can also put a dab of olive oil or holy water in each corner of the room and by any doors or windows.

If you feel threatened at any time while using a Ouija board, order the spirit to go away and stop the Ouija session immediately.

None of these techniques are foolproof and the best way to avoid summoning or inviting a demon is to not use the Ouija board.

A séance gone wrong or held by someone who is not experienced in conducting a séance could also lead to the summoning of a demon.

In my opinion, séances are a little easier to control than using a Ouija board because, in many cases, the people participating in the séance are trying to contact a specific person. However, it is possible for a demon to impersonate someone else, so caution should still be used.

As with a Ouija board, when holding a séance, a prayer of protection should be said before the séance begins, and white candles should be lit and placed on the table.

Some people believe that putting a circle of sea salt around the séance table works at keeping evil spirits away from the séance. I've never personally tried this technique, but it seems reasonable.

You can also use olive oil or holy water in the same manner you would if using a Ouija board.

Again, if you feel scared, threatened, or apprehensive about any spirit that may come through while the séance is going on, order that spirit to leave immediately and, once you're sure it's gone, stop the séance and break the circle.

Another possible way a demon could be summoned or invited into a location is if someone who is mentally and/or emotionally unstable is at that location. To a demon, this would be interpreted as a sign of weakness, and a demon could potentially prey on that person, causing sometimes irreversible damage to that person and the people around them.

Negative emotions such as anger, jealousy, depression, etc., could be attractive targets for a demon. Negativity in an environment filled with a lot of fighting and arguing could draw a demon in.

Just because you or someone in your family didn't summon or invite a demon into your lives doesn't mean one isn't already there. By this I mean that a demon could be in the home you buy, the place you work, or just about anywhere, and you, like me, would be a victim of circumstance. Once a demon is there, it can hang around for days, weeks, years, even centuries, until it is made to leave.

You can smudge your house in an attempt to rid the home of a demon. Smudging is a Native American ritual performed with a smudge stick, generally made up of dried sage and sweet grass; I add a bit of frankincense to mine. This mixture is believed to force any negative energy or beings from a building. Even a person can be smudged.

DEMON OR SPIRIT?

One of the questions I'm most frequently asked is whether demons can physically injure people. In general, demons can inflict physical injuries on people. They are capable of scratching, biting, leaving welts on the body; they can make you feel as if you're being strangled, and in extreme cases, you may wake up feeling as if you were being sexually assaulted.

As I've said before, demons can announce their presence by emitting a foul order that smells a lot like rotten eggs; they can and do scratch on walls, knock on walls, desecrate or move religious objects in your home; and you may hear a low, menacing growl. They are capable of making verbal threats, and they can also hit, shove, push, and scratch.

Many people mistake a common haunting by a ghost or spirit as being a demon. I can't tell you how many times people have called me thinking they have a demon only to learn it's really a ghost or spirit. If you're not sure what you have, you should seek out an experienced paranormal team to help identify what is going on in your home.

As severe as being pushed, shoved, scratched, or tormented sounds, a demon is capable of much worse. Some paranormal investigators believe one way to tell the difference between an angry spirit and a demon is by the severity of the attacks.

An angry spirit can become violent, but generally, if told to stop in a calm, assertive manner, this type of spirit will back off and hide for a few days or weeks, while a demon will escalate the attacks to a higher intensity than before.

An angry spirit may still try to enforce its reign of terror upon the living, but the attacks will not worsen in intensity.

Gaining Control

While demons are more than capable of physical attack, their main weapon is psychological warfare. They seem to have an innate ability to find where a person is the most vulnerable—what their greatest fear is, and/or where they are weak—and target that specific trait.

One of a demon's main goals is to isolate you from your friends, family, co-workers, or anyone else so that the only thing you have to turn to is the demon itself. It wants you to surrender to it.

When a demon is gaining control over your life, it will make things happen around you—like Amon did with my friends—in order to force you to make the choice it wants. In my case, I chose to partially isolate myself from my friends in order to keep them safe by not talking about the Matthews house or the demon.

Some of you may be wondering how it's possible for a demon to gain your trust. I mean any reasonable person would flee at the sight of a demon, right?

The answer is yes, of course, one would run if they knew they were dealing with a demon, but that's the problem—most of the time you won't know. Demons can transform themselves into anything or anyone they choose.

A demon might appear to be the spirit of a child, or a departed friend or family member. They do this to gain your trust and put you off-guard. Then, before you even realize it's happened, the demon has isolated you from friends and family and is firmly in control. By control, I don't mean possession, I mean a demon having some type of outside control of your life, or what you have left of it.

Looking back, I'm now convinced that demons, at the very least this demon, in his own sick and twisted way, played fair; he gave me the choice to walk away. I know there are demonologists out there who may disagree with this premise, and they may be right, but I can only speak to how I felt then, how I feel now, and what I personally experienced.

However, I would argue this: humans have free will, and while a demon could place temptations and/or choices before us, we have the ability to choose our course of action. Demons have had thousands of years to study and learn about human nature and, in my opinion, can predict with relative certainty how the majority of humans will react in certain situations. In other words, a demon is quite adept at psychological warfare, and is capable of waging this type of battle without interfering with our free will.

Many religions believe that a demon's only goal is to turn you away from God. While I respect their beliefs, I'm not sure I totally agree that it's the sole motivation for a demon. In fact, the more I think about it, my demon actually made me turn to God more than I ever have in my life. I am not disagreeing with these religions; I'm simply stating that, for me, I clung to my faith as a means of surviving this encounter with a demon.

Fear is the enemy here. Fear is a negative emotion and literally "feeds" the demon or any negative entity and makes them more powerful. They only become more powerful because we fear them. So the secret is not to show them fear. I know it's easier said than done, but not showing fear may be the only means of survival against them.

It's also my belief that demons can mark you in some way. It's not a physical mark, although they are more than capable of doing that. No, I think they mark your soul and when they do, they can find you again—anytime, anyplace, —and there's nothing you can do to stop it.

There is a school of thought found among paranormal researchers and religions alike that speaking the demon's name will summon the demon to you. I believe the opposite; my belief is that if you do speak the demon's name, it gives you some sort of power over the demon—not much, mind you, but enough to make you feel empowered (the key words being "make you feel").

Demons are capable of letting you think you've gained some measure of power over them, but in reality, you haven't. It's just another illusion to let you think you're still in control.

It's been my experience that when a demon enters your life, it's futile to attempt to gain control over it. What you really want to do is regain control over yourself and get your life back.

Whether you seek the help of clergy or a paranormal investigator who is experienced in dealing with demonic entities, the choice is yours. The main thing to remember is that you're engaged in spiritual warfare and the stakes are the highest they've ever been.

For further reading on demons I recommend *The Encyclopedia of Demons and Demonology* by Rosemary Ellen Guiley.

Signs that a Demon is at Work

When a person is being preyed upon by a demon, you may notice a change in their behavior. The person may start to isolate themselves, or act out in uncharacteristic ways, such as exhibiting violent behavior. They may start drinking alcohol heavily or turn to drugs.

For example, I became withdrawn from my friends and family. I had to physically and emotionally force myself to keep up the appearance of acting as I normally would act, when in truth, I lived, breathed, ate, and slept thinking about Amon. The demon became an obsession. It was no longer about the house or the Matthews family, it was only about Amon.

I've read case studies about others who have encountered demons, but I have not actually met anyone else who experienced what I did; of course, it's not something to be talked about in polite company.

EXORCISMS

No chapter on demons would be complete without a short discussion on exorcism. An exorcism is a specific ritual that is designed to banish a demon from a place or person. While exorcisms are most commonly connected with the Catholic Church, many other religions such as Islam, Judaism, Hinduism, and Buddhism have special rituals to get rid of demons. The practice of exorcism dates back hundreds if not thousands of years.

Before the advancement of psychology, exorcisms were routinely performed to cast out what many perceived as demons when, in reality, the person was simply mentally ill. In modern times exorcisms have been performed less frequently, although the Catholic Church reports that they are once again on the rise throughout the world.

Demonic possession is different from a demonic haunting. In a possession a living human being's body is being occupied by the demon, while in a demonic haunting a specific place is occupied by a demonic entity—although in these cases, the demon tends to pick out a person in that place to try to control without actually possessing them.

Many Catholic exorcists, the people who are charged with getting rid of the possessing demon, are specially trained by the church. The process of exorcising a demon can be long and dangerous, not only for the person who is possessed, but for the exorcist themselves. Some believe that a demon can leave the body of the person they are possessing and enter the exorcist's body.

For the average person, an exorcism would be a very dangerous thing to do without the assistance of someone who understands demons and knows how to get rid of them. The same holds true if you believe your home or place of business is being occupied by a demon.

Taking on a demon is not for the faint of heart or someone who is not mentally and spiritually strong. Demons are capable of many things still not completely understood by the church or many paranormal investigators.

Demons are capable of psychological warfare at a very high level and when a demon possesses a living person it is in total control of that person's mind and body. The demon can and will make someone act out in ways that are totally out of character for that person, and can use that person's body to cause great harm to others.

In a Catholic exorcism many things such as crosses, holy water, and special prayers are used to banish the demon. However, in other Christian religions the "laying on of hands" and prayers are used to "heal" the person who is possessed to get the demon to leave their body.

My question is, where is the demon sent? Do exorcists send it back to the darkness from which it came? Or do they just force the demon out of the possessed body and leave it loose upon the world?

Many of the rites of exorcism I've read generally ask God or whatever supreme power one believes in to assist in getting the demon to leave the possessed person, which is the goal of the exorcism. But few send the demon back to the place from which it came.

BE CAREFUL WHAT YOU WISH FOR

It never ceases to amaze me how some people who have paranormal activity in their house automatically jump to the conclusion that it's being caused by a demon; and they say it excitedly, like they want it to be a demon.

Trust me—no one wants a demon in their home or their lives. Yet people seem fascinated by demons and are sometimes disappointed when I tell them that they have a ghost, not a demon.

Some of these people even keep insisting it's a demon in their home, and they wear it like a badge of honor. It's this type of behavior that can draw a demon into their lives and create a living nightmare. So a word of caution: be careful what you wish for.

For further reading I'd recommend "Beating a Demon: Physical Dimensions of Spiritual Warfare," by Bobby Jindal, *New Oxford Review* (December 1994), http://newpoliticus

.blogspot.com/2009/03/beating-demon-physical-dimensions-of.html; or *The Dark Sacrament: True Stories of Modern-Day Demon Possession and Exorcism* by David M. Kiely and Christina McKenna (New York: HarperOne, 2008).

So now that you know a little bit about demons, it's time to begin my story. There may be some who don't believe this story, some who even say I'm making the whole thing up. That is their choice. They can believe what they want, and they can deny the existence of demons. I'm okay with that.

CHAPTER TWO

I wasn't looking for trouble the first day I ran into the house on the hill. I'd been wishing for a new adventure—something exciting. The whole thing started the summer my twins graduated from high school and went out on their own—my son went into the armed services and my daughter moved in with a friend of hers.

My husband and I bought a brand-new house in a rather rural part of the Northwest. We liked the fact that this place had a small-town atmosphere and a boating community—we're avid boaters.

While we were sad to leave our old house and our friends, we were both excited about moving into our new house. We used to drive through the area when the twins were little, dreaming about the time we could afford to move out there. Now, twenty-five years later, our dream became a reality.

We settled in nicely, and I spent the first few months buying furniture, decorating, and getting acclimated to the new surroundings. But soon boredom set in, and because I didn't know a single person in my new town, I decided to join the Historical Society since I've always loved history.

It was close to Halloween and the Historical Society was having a candlelight walk through the quaint little town. I decided to attend. I arrived at the Historical Museum in the center of town in the early evening. The night was clear and chilly, but a light fog rolled in off the lake, giving the town an eerie feel.

The Historical Museum was housed in what used to be a brothel-turned-hotel-turned-boarding house. I greeted several people and made my way through the museum, which was decorated with Victorian-era furniture, to get my candle and cup of hot apple cider. I stood at a large dining room table looking over all the baked goods, deciding what I wanted, when I noticed a large picture hanging on the wall.

"I wonder who that is?" I said.

"Robert Matthews," a voice beside me answered.

I turned to see a short, heavyset woman in her late forties with curly gray and black hair standing next to me.

"Who's he?" I asked.

"He was a state senator and did a lot of good things for the town," the woman answered with a slight Southern drawl. "My name's Susan."

I introduced myself and we shook hands.

"Interesting picture," I said, walking over to get a closer look.

The portrait was of a man with fair skin and light-colored hair. His eyes seemed to follow me around the room, and I couldn't help but notice the energy emanating from the painting. It felt as if the spirit of the man was *in* the painting. The feeling caused me to shiver slightly.

"You're psychic," Susan said, not as a question but as a statement of fact. Her green eyes met mine and I could tell this curious woman didn't miss much.

"Yes, but how did you know?" I stammered.

"By the way you reacted to the picture. Kinda spooky, isn't it?" Susan chuckled. Her voice and laugh reminded me of that woman in the movie *Poltergeist*.

"It is," I agreed.

"We should probably go outside and get ready for the walk, and I want to have a cigarette. Do you have a lighter?" Susan asked, searching her coat pockets.

"Sure. Come on." My new friend and I walked out in front of the museum and sat on a wooden bench to have a smoke.

"You're new here, aren't you? I haven't seen you before and I know just about everyone," Susan said, taking a long drag on her cigarette.

"Yes. I just moved here a few months ago. You're the first person I've met."

Susan grabbed my hand. "You and I—we're going to be good friends. I can tell. I believe in ghosts, you know. I've had lots of experiences I can't wait to tell you about. Come on. Let's get in line for the walk."

The president of the Historical Society was a rotund man wearing a black coat and a large top hat. His booming, cheerful voice guided us through town. He talked about the history of some of the buildings along with the ghost stories that shrouded the small lakeside town in mystique.

As we strolled by an empty lot, I "saw" an old meat counter and bakery and, without thinking, walked into the now-vacant lot to explore some more.

"Did this used to be a meat market?" I asked.

The president of the Historical Society, Fred, turned around and looked at me.

"Why would you say that?" he asked.

"Because I see an old meat counter and scales over here. But I'm confused, because I see a bar over here," I said.

"After the meat market moved to another store, a bar took over the space. That could account for your confusion. What else do you see?" he asked.

By this time the rest of the people on the walk had gathered in the empty lot.

"I see a fire. A big fire. It's everywhere, almost the entire town," I answered.

"Yes. There was a huge fire that almost burned down the entire town," Fred said.

"What else do you see?" someone in the crowd asked.

"Well," I said tentatively. I hate being the center of attention. "I see people dressed in Victorian clothing walking down the sidewalk. The men dressed in their finery with pocket watches and canes and the ladies carrying parasols. They aren't really here, you know, it's just the residual energy of days gone by that I'm seeing. Also, when we passed the last building I saw two men in period dress arguing. That's about it."

"Could you recognize the men if you saw them again?" Fred asked.

"Yes," I answered, noticing that the crowd of people was getting closer. I backed up a couple of steps.

Susan walked over and put a protective arm around my shoulder. "That's enough for now," she said. "Alexis is new in town and we don't want to scare her off now, do we?" Susan narrowed her eyes at the crowd.

"Yes, of course," Fred said. "Let's keep going, shall we?"

When we returned to the front of the museum, Fred told us about Robert Matthews and his family. They moved here from out East and built a mansion just outside of town.

Robert's son, Jacob, had a daughter named Mary Elizabeth who died under "mysterious circumstances" after being married only a short time. According to Fred, their mansion was one of the most haunted places around.

He went on to tell us that there had been reports of footsteps going up and down the staircase. In one instance, an older couple pulled into the driveway of the house and saw the ghost of a little girl, who told them to get out. The couple was scared so badly they ran a stop sign on the way home. Fred also said that a psychic once went to the house and ran out the door a few minutes later, vowing never to set foot in the house again. To this day, the psychic hasn't told a soul about what happened to her in the house.

The house was sold in the early 1900s by Jacob's widow after Robert and Jacob died. A woman bought it and turned it into a bed and breakfast; she added an addition to the house, which brought the total square footage to six thousand.

Of course, I instantly became fascinated with the story of the Matthews family.

After the walk concluded, Fred pulled me aside and showed me an old photo album. He flipped through the pages and stopped at the third page.

"Do you recognize anyone?" he asked.

"This man. He was one of the men arguing at that building." I pointed to a photo of a distinguished man with dark hair and a beard.

"That's Ephrium Losch. He was one of the founders of the town. That building used to be his office. I think the other man you saw might have been Jacob Matthews. Aaccording to some newspaper accounts, they clashed heads a few times in public."

Susan and I chatted with Fred and a few other townsfolk before extracting ourselves from the museum.

"Do you want to go have some coffee and chat?" Susan asked.

I readily agreed and followed Susan to a cute little restaurant. We settled into a booth with a cup of hot coffee. After ordering something to eat, Susan and I began to chat.

I learned she had two daughters, both grown, and one granddaughter. Her husband of twenty-four years worked and wasn't home much. Sounded like my life.

"How did you like the candlelight walk?" Susan asked, wrapping her hands around her coffee cup to warm them.

"It was really good. Wish he'd said more about the Matthews house though," I sighed.

Susan laughed. "I know all about that house. Friends of mine, Dan and Lisa, own the place."

"Really? Have they had anything happen?"

"Yeah. My husband, Bob, was helping them do demolition on the house. They wanted to turn it back into a bed and breakfast. Bob said they would hear footsteps, like someone walking up and down the stairs with a cane. Dan and Lisa lived in the apartment at the back of the house for five or six years, but don't anymore."

"Why did they move out?" I asked.

"They got divorced. But soon after they started demolition, my daughter and Dan were involved in a really bad car accident that almost killed them both. It took about a year for Dan to recover and no work got done on the house."

"Wow, are they okay now?"

"Yeah, they're fine." Susan smiled.

"That's great," I said.

"Thank you."

Susan wrinkled her forehead up in thought. "You know, when they started working on the house again, my husband told me something really strange happened to him and Dan."

"Oh yeah?" I answered. "What happened?"

"They were scared out of the house when they were working on the furnace in the basement. They couldn't find any reason why the furnace wouldn't work. Anyway, they heard a deep voice. It yelled at them to get out. It happened a couple of times, and then they would hear something growl. They dropped their tools and ran out of the house." Susan chuckled. "They went back to the house about an hour later and the same thing happened again, so they gave up. Wimps," Susan said with a gleam in her eye.

"I've got to get into this house," I told Susan.

"We can go tomorrow if you want. Lisa lives next door to me and I can get the key from her," Susan said.

After paying our bill, Susan and I exchanged telephone numbers and addresses and made plans for me to have breakfast at her house the next morning before going to the Matthews house.

As I drove home from the restaurant, I thought about what Susan told me about the house. I'd run across malevolent ghosts before, but this one sounded, by all accounts, pretty nasty. A sense of anticipation filled my body.

When I got home I took a hot, cleansing bath with a custom mixture of sea salt, dried rosemary, and sage to wash away any negative energy that may have been clinging to me. Before I went to sleep I meditated on the day to come and used the meditation to make sure my gifts were fine-tuned and ready to go. I know now that no amount of preparation would have prepared me for the events that were to follow.

Now that I've had the last few years to think about the events Susan told me about, it's possible that the car accident was just that—an accident. But considering all the other events Dan and Lisa experienced in that house, it wouldn't be a stretch to attribute the accident to the demon because, according to my research, demons try to be as disruptive as possible.

Bob and Dan's experience when working on the furnace could also be attributed to the demon, especially the growling. The furnace was located in the same room where I believe the demon's nest was, and the demon would do just about anything to keep people away from its nest. In fact, the more I've thought about it, the luckier I think Bob and Dan were. A demon is capable of horrific violence, and was actually, in its own way, playing fair by warning Bob and Dan to get out of there.

CHAPTER THREE

The next morning, instead of taking the main roads, Susan suggested I take a shortcut. As I drove along, I paid attention to everything on this unfamiliar road. I passed an old cemetery that caught my interest and made a mental note to visit it as soon as possible. I kept driving, curiously peering out the windshield at the homes and other places of interest.

Suddenly, I ran headfirst into a wall of energy. I felt like I was running full speed into a brick wall. Without thinking, I slammed on the brakes, sending a shower of dust and gravel spiraling around my Jeep. I quickly checked my rearview mirror and was grateful no one was behind me.

"What the hell was that?" I gasped.

After catching my breath, I looked around to see where the sudden blast of energy came from. That's when I saw it—the house on the hill. That's how the townsfolk commonly referred to the Matthews house.

The house itself, an imposing structure, seemed to have thrust itself out of the earth and made me feel like it defied anyone to venture between its walls. The old red brick of the 1800s wrapped itself around the house like a protective shield.

The house stood three stories tall and had huge two-story bay windows jutting out from the front. I couldn't wait for the opportunity to explore the depths of the old Victorian home later that morning.

As beautiful as the home was, it still did nothing to explain the wall of energy that had smacked me hard upside the head. Because I've experienced running into a wall of energy on one or two paranormal investigations, I knew enough to immediately put a protective shield of energy around myself to keep any other energy out. Doing this allows me to regroup. While it's not really scary running into this type of energy, it does kick my curiosity into high gear. I realize now that was my first warning; one I obviously chose to ignore.

Shaking off the residual feelings of energy, I continued on my way to Susan's. As I drove, I thought about what had just happened. I've run into energy like that on other investigations for a few different reasons—either a spirit is trying to get my attention, is scared, or doesn't want me there for whatever reason. When a spirit or other type of entity puts up a wall of energy as strong as the one I encountered that day, I consider it an act of aggression or an attempt to protect itself. I then proceed with caution.

As I drove, I couldn't decide whether the entity that threw up that wall of energy was acting in an aggressive manner or defending its turf. Either way, I didn't have to wait long to find out which one it was.

A few minutes later I pulled into Susan's driveway and she welcomed me into her well-kept two-story colonial. We settled ourselves at the kitchen table to eat breakfast, and I told her about what happened on the way to her house.

"Interesting," Susan said. "What do you think it means?"

"I'm not sure," I shrugged. "But I felt like the house was trying to suck me in, like a giant vacuum."

Susan laughed. "I know how that feels. I've been drawn to Mary Elizabeth's grave ever since I moved here twelve years ago. She's buried in the cemetery just down the street from the house. In the summer I sit by her grave and crochet and talk to her."

"Why do you think you're drawn to her grave?" I asked. I took another bite of the amazing biscuits and gravy Susan had prepared for breakfast. I could feel my arteries clog as I chewed, but the flavors were irresistible.

"I think it's because I'm so curious about how she died. I mean, 'mysterious circumstances,' what the hell is that? I guess I'm hoping one day she will talk back to me," Susan explained, as she busied herself with pouring us more coffee.

I nodded. "It is a mystery. When did she die?"

"Spring of 1881," Susan answered.

"So, she's been dead almost a hundred and ten years and the town's still talking about it, if the conversation after the candlelight walk is any indication. Everyone was talking about Mary Elizabeth and the Matthews family." I sipped my coffee.

"Yeah. It's like this whole town knows a secret and won't share it." Susan paused with a forkful of food halfway to her mouth. "I've been asking about the Matthews family for years, and no one will answer my questions. Somebody knows something, I'm convinced of it. I'm sure they think I'm just a crazy old bitch." Susan chortled.

"Well, I believe you, so looks like this small town is now going to have to contend with two crazy old bitches." I giggled.

"Good," Susan laughed, rising from her chair to start clearing the table.

After cleaning up the breakfast dishes, Susan and I got into my Jeep and headed over to the Matthews house.

"The house is in pretty rough shape," Susan explained as we drove. "There are a few pieces of furniture in it, but Dan and Lisa have pretty much gutted the place down to the studs. They were planning on rewiring and updating the heating system, but then they split up."

"So there's no heat or electricity?" I asked.

"There's electricity on in part of the house, like the basement and the apartment they used to live in, but nowhere else. There should be enough light coming through the windows for us to see okay, but if we come here at night we're going to have to bring flashlights," Susan said.

We arrived at the house a few minutes later and I eagerly leapt from the truck. As we walked towards the house I kept anticipating running into the wall of energy I'd felt earlier, but it instead felt like the house had reabsorbed the energy and was anticipating our arrival.

The house seemed to pulsate with energy; it was almost palpable. The pounding in my ears in the rhythm of a heartbeat made me stop to see if it was mine. It wasn't. This feeling only fanned the flames of curiosity that were racing through my body.

To this day, I would swear in open court on a stack of bibles that the house had a soul. It was alive and would use any means at its disposal to protect itself and the secrets that lay within its walls.

Normally, when I investigate a new location, I rush right in and go to every room so I can get a layout of the place in my head. Then I go back and explore the place very slowly, room by room.

Not this time. The energy of the once-grand mansion made me want to savor every second in the house.

The grandeur and beauty of the home, although faded and worn, were still apparent. The peeling hunter green paint on the trim around the windows, the faded and cracked red brick of the exterior, and the large well-used rounded steps and faded wooden floor boards of the front porch told the whole story—the once glorious home had fallen into a state of neglect and was showing its age.

"When was this house built?" I asked.

"No one's really sure. Some records say 1843, but others say 1857," Susan answered.

Susan and I fell into a companionable silence as we walked around the outside of the house, peering in the windows that were low enough for us to reach. We saw an old cistern filled with discarded building materials through one of the basement windows, and we almost stepped into an old well someone had filled with stones.

Squirrels were scampering around us gathering acorns, and birds were singing their morning song to each other in the trees. I could hear the traffic from the main road whizzing by, yet it felt as if I'd entered a bubble that seemed to encapsulate the house, trapping it in the past.

It didn't take long to figure out the dividing line between the three-story addition and the original footprint of the house. The brick was slightly different and the top part of the addition was covered with faded white aluminum siding.

I also noticed a big difference between the addition and the other part of the house. The original home felt charged with energy, while the addition didn't appear to throw out any energy I could feel.

This actually gave me a lot of information about any ghosts that occupied the property. Most of the time, a ghost will totally ignore an addition to a home because it wasn't there when they were alive. The fact that all the energy was coming from the original part of the house told me that whatever ghosts were awaiting us inside died before the addition was added in the early 1900s.

When I reached the front of the house I tentatively stepped on the first of four steps leading to the front door.

The old wood floorboards felt a little soft under my feet, but supported my weight. I let my hand skim the paint-flaked railing as I climbed the remaining steps. The sunlight filtering through the branches of the giant fir trees cast eerie shadows on the porch as I made my way to the front door.

I reached my hand out to touch the worn brass doorknob and, just as my hand curled around it, I heard a deep, loud, throaty growl that seemed to come from the other side of the door. Instinctively, I jerked my hand away and took a couple of steps backwards.

"Susan, do Dan and Lisa have a dog in the house?" I asked.

"No, they don't even own a dog. Besides, the house is empty. Why?" Susan said.

After telling her what happened, we both spread out and looked for a dog anywhere in the immediate area. We came up empty.

It wasn't until much later, when I took the time to replay everything in my head, that I remembered it got very quiet when I started to walk up the stairs to the front porch, which was extremely strange.

Even though the house sat about five hundred feet off the two main roads, traffic could still be heard quite clearly. The lot the house sat on covered almost an acre and fairly populated with large mature trees. The sound of birds singing and flitting in and out of the branches, as well as the sound of squirrels, of which there were many, racing around property gathering food for the coming winter completely stopped. There was complete silence.

At first blush, one could surmise that, because the front door of the home was tucked deep in between the massive bay windows, the noise was somehow muffled, or buffered altogether. I believe this was my second warning, one I didn't even acknowledge.

While a demon is capable of making the surrounding area deadly quiet, so are some ghosts and had I noticed the silence at the time, I would have chalked it up to ghost activity.

Shrugging off the strange event, Susan extracted a key from the pocket of her jeans and we entered the house through a side door located in the addition portion of the home.

This entrance opened immediately into a small, run-down apartment with a studio kitchen/dining area, living room, and small hallway that led to a rather cramped bedroom.

Susan led the way through the living room towards the door that joined the apartment to the original portion of the home.

"Wow," I said, stopping just short of the door leading to the main house.

"What?" Susan asked, turning around. Her green eyes were focused on me.

"The apartment doesn't really have any energy to speak of, but as we get closer to the older section of the house, the energy is becoming very intense," I said.

"Maybe the ghosts are coming to greet you," Susan suggested as she crossed the threshold into the oldest part of the home.

"Could be." I hesitated before stepping through the doorway to follow Susan, who'd already walked halfway up a long hallway towards the front door.

After crossing the threshold, I felt dizzy and disoriented. It was the same energy I'd felt on the way to Susan's earlier that morning. I reached out to steady myself against one of the only remaining wet-plaster walls in the house. I took a few deep breaths and allowed my energy vibrations to automatically adjust to the ones in the home.

"Are you okay?" Susan rushed to my side.

"I'll be fine," I assured her. "Ghosts have energy vibrations, like radio frequencies, and it takes me a couple of minutes to adjust my energy to match theirs. Until I make that adjustment I sometimes get dizzy."

"Do you want to leave?" Concern filled Susan's face.

"It would take an act of God to get me to leave this house," I said.

We both laughed and, within a matter of seconds, the dizziness disappeared and my head cleared enough for me to focus on the house itself.

Susan and I made our way up the long hallway ahead of us and I saw the wall that encased the stairway leading to the upper floors to my left.

"This floor still has most of the original walls," Susan explained. "But the upper floors are gutted down to the studs."

"Let's go check out the front door. I want to figure out what that growling sound was," I said.

Susan and I made a beeline for the front door and tried everything we could think of to duplicate the noise, but we were unable to.

"The front door is nailed shut and pieces of wood are bolted across it," Susan said as she examined the door. "We couldn't open this door an inch even if we wanted to, and I don't see anything that could have made that growling sound you heard."

"Me either. Maybe one of the ghosts was trying to scare us away," I suggested.

"Like that's going to happen." Susan giggled.

"Amen to that, sister." I laughed. We high-fived each other and walked into the room to the right of the foyer where a large fireplace sat on the far outside wall. The room was bathed in early morning sunlight that came through the huge bay window. The well-worn original hardwood floors still showed signs of the dark, rich varnish that once made them gleam.

"Oh wow!" I said, rushing to the middle of the room. "Look! Pocket doors!" I carefully eased one of the large doors out of its slot and slid it across half the room.

"This must have been the parlors," Susan said, looking around. "The pocket doors would have been used to separate the men's parlor from the women's parlor because back in the old days it wasn't polite for a man to smoke a cigar in front of a woman."

"You're probably right." I carefully slid the door back in its place.

"I'm going to the room across the hall. Give you a chance to do what you do."

"Okay. Thanks," I said, and watched Susan disappear across the foyer into the next room.

I walked slowly around the room, allowing myself to feel the energy and put out feelers for possible ghosts or spirits who may have been in the room with me. Oddly enough, the room felt relatively normal, except for one spot located by the bay window at the front of the house. When I stood in that spot I felt a burst of energy around me.

"Hey, Susan," I called out. "Come here for a second."

Susan rejoined me in the parlor.

"There's some really weird energy right here," I said, furrowing my brow.

"What does it feel like?" Susan walked over to stand by me. "I don't have a psychic bone in my body."

"It doesn't feel like a spirit, this is different. I've never felt anything like it," I said. "It feels hot and cold at the same time and the energy feels dark and heavy. Something doesn't want us here and it's letting us know in a very passive-aggressive way. I've never felt anything like this before," I said.

"What do you mean?"

"I mean, if a negative or dark energy wants you gone, it will become very aggressive and could throw something at you, push you, scratch you, whatever. But this energy is coming up through the floor and is just strong enough to let me know it's there. It's giving us a chance to back off and leave. What's under this room?" I said.

"The basement, but I'm not sure it goes under this room. We'll check it out later. I'm going to take some pictures of the dining room across the hall." Susan pulled a digital camera out of her jacket pocket.

"I'll be there in a minute."

Susan walked out of the room and a few seconds later I could hear the click of her camera as she squeezed off shots.

I made my way back to the foyer. My tennis shoes barely made any noise on the dark, varnished hardwood floors. The original planked wood doors were still in place on the entrance to the parlor and dining room, but sometime over the years they'd been painted bright white.

I noticed the hand-carved cove moldings that separated the walls from the ceiling throughout the first floor, but they, too, had been painted. It seemed almost offensive to me; I could see where the paint was chipped and peeled, revealing that, at one time, the moldings were varnished a rich mahogany color. In its day, the house must have been a showplace and home to a family of high society and wealth.

As I walked by the front door to join Susan in the dining room, I swear I heard an audible voice softly say, "Welcome home, I've been waiting for you."

While those words now send chills up my spine, at the time I found them a comfort. Being adopted—coupled with my psychic abilities—I've always felt out of place, like I really didn't fit in anywhere. So to have a place welcome me home and make me have a sense of belonging was a big deal.

What I didn't realize when I heard the voice welcome me home was that it was just the first step by the demon to gain my trust, for lack of a better word. It was as if, in an instant, this creature was able to pinpoint my one weakness and prey upon it without a moment's hesitation. It did so in such a way that I let my guard down.

My natural curiosity took over and I eagerly began to explore every nook and cranny of the house. When I'm relaxed, my gifts tend to shift into overdrive and give me a lot more information.

"Are you picking anything else up?" Susan asked as she joined me in the foyer.

For the first time since entering the property I began to focus on what the house was ready to reveal to me. I turned my attention to the staircase that wound up the center of the house like a viper.

"I see a young woman in a Victorian dress tumble down the stairs and land in a crumpled heap on the floor right here." I pointed to a spot on the floor in front of me. "That means two things. First, a young woman died here and it's residual energy, meaning I'm just seeing the energy of what happened. The ghost isn't here. It's like a piece of time gets stuck in a time warp and replays itself over and over."

"Mary Elizabeth," Susan whispered, almost reverently. "It all makes sense now."

I nodded as we both fell silent, remembering that the president of the Historical Society told us of how Mary Elizabeth had died under mysterious circumstances.

"You know," Susan said, turning to face me. "There are some people I know who said something's tried to push them down the stairs when they were going up to the third floor. My daughter was pregnant and something tried to push her down the stairs here too."

"Really? That means there must be an intelligent spirit on the third floor," I mused.

"Intelligent?" Susan asked.

"Yes. An intelligent entity is a ghost or spirit that interacts with the living in some way, unlike residual energy that doesn't acknowledge the living. So now the question becomes, is the spirit trying to push people down the stairs to frighten them out of the house, or is it trying to push people down the stairs to tell us what happened to Mary Elizabeth?" I thought aloud.

"Could be either," Susan said. "I think we need to head up to the third floor."

We trudged up the staircase to the second floor, but I didn't feel the presence of any type of entity, so we slowly began to ascend the staircase to the third floor with me leading the way, both of us careful to cling tightly to the handrail.

Halfway up the stairs I felt the energy change abruptly. Then, I became aware of a presence at the top of the stairs.

"There's someone standing on the landing," I whispered to Susan.

"Who is it?"

"I don't know yet. It doesn't feel threatening, but I haven't felt this energy anywhere else in the house. Hang back a step or two just in case," I said.

Susan stopped where she was, and I continued up the stairs. When I got two steps from the landing I felt two unseen hands rest against my shoulders and give me a slight shove—not hard enough to push me down the stairs, but strong enough to get my attention.

"Back off!" I commanded.

CHAPTER FOUR

The spirit obliged quickly. I felt that it wasn't expecting any-one to communicate with it, which isn't unusual. Very few people try to communicate with spirits; normally they just run in fear. The rapid retreat of the spirit told me that I'd probably scared it and it ran away to regroup.

"What happened?!?" Susan asked.

"A ghost just shoved me a little—I think it was to scare me, not hurt me. It's okay, it's scurried off somewhere," I assured her.

Susan laughed. "It was probably surprised someone stood up to it."

"Maybe," I agreed.

Susan and I climbed the last couple of steps to the vast expanse of the third floor. All that was left of the walls were the roughly cut studs and the rough brick of the outside walls. The original doors were hanging on their hinges and had also been painted white. As we walked around, I noticed an extremely narrow staircase to the right of the main stairway that led up to the cupola.

Susan busied herself by going from room to room, snapping photographs to see if she could get any pictures of ghosts, while I went in search of the entity that tried to shove me down the stairs.

I wandered aimlessly through the space, keeping myself open to the energy of the house and the entity. I discovered that when I went through the doorway from the original part of the house to the addition, the energy changed as it had before.

"Hey, Susan, where are you?" I called.

"I'm right here," Susan said, walking to the rear of the third floor to join me.

"You know, whatever paranormal activity is taking place in the house is contained to the older section, and the newer section is acting as sort of a neutral zone. The ghosts won't go into the addition."

"Really? So what does that mean?" Susan asked.

"It means that because the addition wasn't added to the house until the early 1900s, any ghosts were here before the addition was added."

"So ..." Susan said.

"So, many ghosts and spirits won't acknowledge an addition or something that wasn't here when they were alive. There have been thousands of cases where people report seeing ghosts walk through walls. In most of those cases the house has been remodeled and the ghost is simply walking through what used to be a doorway when they were alive."

"Oh, I get it," Susan said. "So does that mean the ghosts are residual?"

"Not really. While normally this type of activity is associated with a residual haunting, there are always exceptions," I answered.

"Interesting," Susan said, as she wandered away. "I'm going to finish taking pictures."

Once Susan finished taking pictures we made our way up the narrow staircase to the cupola. The view from up there was amazing. The town, once a main shipping port, was now but a sleepy little hamlet.

"Do you remember what Fred told us on the candlelight walk?" Susan asked.

"About the house?"

"Remember he told us that Jacob Matthews spent hours up here with binoculars watching their fleet of schooners come into port at the Matthews's docks," Susan said.

"Yeah, I can see why. This view is awesome."

We stared out the windows of the cupola, both lost in our own thoughts.

"You know, when my husband Bob was working on the demolition here, he complained that tools kept disappearing and would show up a day or two later, right where he left them. And again, Dan, Lisa, and Bob have all told me that they kept hearing footsteps on the stairway, like someone walking with a cane going up or down the stairs."

"Cool," I said.

As we talked, we made our way back down the narrow staircase to the third floor. When we got to the landing, I began to walk through the rooms and Susan started taking more pictures.

"It's here," I whispered.

"What's here?" Susan asked.

"The ghost who tries to push people down the stairs," I replied, recognizing the energy.

"Where?" Susan answered, looking around the space as if she was expecting to see someone else with us.

"Take a picture of me," I said.

Susan took a couple of pictures and looked at the tiny screen to see if anything out of the ordinary showed up.

"Hey, come look at this," Susan said.

I walked over and peered at the screen. In the picture, a white mist completely surrounded me. While the mist wasn't visible to the naked eye, the camera, using the flash, had no trouble picking up the image.

"Keep taking pictures," I told Susan. Then I asked the spirit, "Are you still here?" I knew a spirit was there; I could feel it, but got no response.

I walked away from Susan as I talked. I could hear the distinct click of her camera and saw the light from the flash every time she squeezed off another shot.

"It's following you," Susan told me, checking each picture in the screen of her camera.

Susan and I continued to take pictures on the third floor for another half hour or so. In the pictures she took of me, the misty, ghostlike figure seemed to be following me around like a puppy dog, except when I went into the addition—then the entity would patiently wait until I returned to the original part of the house.

The entity following me around didn't feel aggressive or mean. I felt feelings of curiosity coming from the unknown ghost. My guess was that no one had tried to communicate with it in many years, and I showed none of the fear that others had when it tried to push them down the stairs.

We wanted to stay in the house longer, but it was almost lunchtime and we both had to get home. Before we left, we decided to check out the only place in the home we hadn't been—the basement.

We wound our way back down the staircase to the first floor and walked through what used to be the kitchen to get to the small set of stairs that led to the basement. It took a couple of minutes to locate the right light switch for the lone light, which did little to illuminate the stairwell, but we made our way cautiously down the well-worn set of stairs.

Susan and I discovered there was only one light in the basement that worked, but the tall basement windows allowed enough sunlight to filter in so we could navigate our way through most of the rooms.

The room to the right of the stairs held shelf after shelf of ceramic molds of all shapes and sizes.

"All these molds were here when Dan and Lisa bought the house," Susan said.

"They're really interesting," I commented as we wandered through the maze of metal shelving units, examining the various molds.

There had to be over a hundred different molds used for statues and ceramic figurines and bowls. There were molds for angels, various animals, religious figures, and molds for making statue bases and other interesting shapes we couldn't identify.

"You name it, there's probably a mold for it somewhere down here." Susan laughed.

"I wonder why they were left here? They have to be worth a small fortune."

"I don't know." Susan shook her head. "But they're amazing."

We ventured through a couple of large empty rooms and noticed a row of smaller rooms that ran through the center of the basement. We walked into the first of these rooms and darkness enveloped us within seconds; we had to feel our way back to the door.

"Hey, I think I remember seeing a flashlight in the apartment. I'll go get it," Susan offered.

"Sounds like a plan." I watched Susan disappear up the stairs to retrieve it.

While I waited for her to return, I decided to explore the room to the left of the staircase. I thought it odd that it was the only room in the basement with a dirt floor; all the others were concrete. I'd felt an energy coming from that room when we'd gotten to the bottom of the stairs that I wanted to check out.

The rather large room had the furnace and water heater at one end, and I noticed a gaping hole in the wall at the other end of the room.

"It must lead to the area underneath the front porch," I said aloud. "But why?"

I started to walk across the room when a wave of energy hit me hard. Before I could decipher what I was feeling, everything in front of my eyes went pure red, then bright white. I couldn't see a thing! All I felt was sheer terror and something else I didn't want to take the time to figure out because I knew if I didn't get out of that room, out of that house—now—something really bad was going to happen.

I backed up a few steps and got my vision to clear before racing up the basement stairs, through the first floor to the apartment, and out the side door into the fresh, fall air.

I sat down on one of the cement stairs leading up to the side door to catch my breath and clear my head. I struggled to stop shaking. I'd never felt anything like that before.

"What happened?" Susan asked, concern filling her green eyes. "You ran out of the house like you'd been shot out of a cannon."

"The room, to the left of the stairs, the one with the dirt floor," I gasped. "There's something really bad in there."

"That's the same room where something yelled at Dan and Bob to get out of the basement when they were fixing the furnace. Remember?" Susan said.

I nodded. "It's also right below the front parlor where I felt that strange energy coming up through the floor."

"You're right," Susan said. "What do you think it is?"

"I don't know, but whatever it is, it's really nasty," I said, shaking my head. "It's also the same energy I ran into on the way to your place—I recognize the energy signature."

"You wait here. I'm going to lock up the house and then we'll go back to my place and look at these pictures on the computer," Susan suggested.

"Sounds good," I agreed. "I also want to go past the cemetery where Mary Elizabeth is buried."

"We can do that tomorrow," Susan said while she locked up the house. I walked to my Jeep and climbed into the driver's seat. I sat staring at the house, trying to get what I'd experienced in the basement to make sense.

That night, we went back to take some pictures of the outside of the Matthews house. When we reviewed the photos from both the inside and outside of the house, we found many interesting anomalies.

In one of the pictures taken on the third floor, a mist was not only wrapped around me, but trailing off to form what looked like an old-fashioned wheelchair. We knew from the candlelight walk that Jacob, who suffered from rheumatoid arthritis, was confined to a wheelchair the last few years of his life. Could this be Jacob trying to tell us it was him? It's not unusual for a spirit to do something like that in order to provide validation of their identity. Susan and I couldn't come up with any other possible explanation.

I'm sure there are some people who would look at that picture and dismiss it as dust because of the condition of the home. These people are, of course, entitled to their opinion, but the picture before and after it were completely void of any trace of what showed up in that photograph. Susan was snapping pictures in very rapid succession as well, so if it was dust, it should have shown up in the picture immediately before and/or after it.

In examining the picture, Susan and I could make out the rough outline of a person who appeared to be a man, standing next to me.

One of the pictures taken in front of the house appeared to have an entity that resembled an angel in it. We saw a beautiful pair of wings attached to what appeared to be some type of entity.

We showed this picture to many people who almost all said they thought it might be an angel, but weren't exactly sure.

But now that a number of years have passed and I reflect on the events of those years and revisit the pictures, I see what is really present in this picture and I have to admit it sends a chill down my spine. The wings were what I let fool me. In addition, no one is sure angels have wings; we only have artists' depictions of what angels may look like. In reality, early artists never painted wings on angels.

Now when I look at the picture, I can clearly see that it is the demon. There appears to be a long snout, like a wolf or some other beast, and an arm that is bent across a rather large body.

In another photograph, also taken that night, Susan swears there is an image of a person standing next to me in the picture, although towering above me height-wise. Considering I'm only five feet tall, that's not hard to do. I have to admit, it does resemble a person, but what I found most interesting was the denseness and amount of ectoplasmic mist that appeared in this picture. It's so thick, I'm barely visible.

Late that evening after first visiting the house on the hill, I took a break from my research into the Matthews family and wandered restlessly through my house. My four cats and my husband were peacefully sleeping and the house was finally quiet.

As I descended the staircase from my office on the second floor of my home, I noticed a massive gray wolf curled up sleeping on the landing of the stairway. I stopped mid-step. It took me a few seconds to realize the wolf wasn't of this world, but was in spirit form.

He opened his beautiful golden eyes and looked at me; our eyes locked. After what seemed like forever, but was really only about a minute, the wolf faded away.

As I watched the wolf disappear, I couldn't help but wonder if this was the beast that growled at me from behind the door of the Matthews house earlier that day.

My initial reaction was that the gray wolf was an animal totem or animal spirit guide there to protect me. The wolf as an animal totem gives us inner strength and teaches us to trust our instincts. They help us take control of our lives. So this would make sense given the situation I didn't even realize I was in at the time.

I shook my head and added the wolf to the ever-growing list of things to figure out.

CHAPTER FIVE

I didn't find out until I started writing this book about the other events that took place in the Matthews house. Susan thought she'd related them to me but hadn't. I'm relaying, in its entirety, a conversation I had with Susan when we met for coffee a few weeks ago.

"I told you about the time Dan and Lisa purchased the new swing, right?" Susan asked as we poured sugar and cream in our coffee and perused the menu.

"No, you didn't. What about the swing?" I asked.

"Oh my God, if I didn't tell you about the swing, then there's a whole lot more to the story than you know about," Susan gasped.

"So tell me now," I said.

"Okay. Anyway, Dan and Lisa bought one of those swings. You know the ones with the free-standing frame and two-person seat that's attached by thick chains."

I nodded.

"Well, they put the swing outside by the apartment entrance under that big tree so it would be in the shade. We were at Lisa and Dan's for a barbeque along with some other people. I was sitting in the swing talking to one of Dan's friends, Larry. We were just gently gliding the swing back and forth when suddenly both chains broke and the swing fell to the ground. Larry broke his leg and my hips were really bruised."

"Oh my God! Did you look at the chains afterwards?"

"Yes, the swing was less than a week old and when we looked at the chain, it didn't look like it broke, but it looked like the links in the chain had been taken apart."

"That's strange," I shook my head.

"I know. We could see scratches in the metal where the links came apart, like someone had used tools to disconnect the links. But wanna hear something else strange?" Susan asked.

"Sure."

"Well, Dan was always a great guy, you know? Kind, friendly, but about a year after they bought the Matthews house, Lisa and I noticed that Dan's behavior began to change."

"Change how?" I asked.

"He became mean. Angry. Hostile. It started out slowly and, at first, Lisa and I thought it was just the stress of trying to remodel the house. But over the next couple of months, he got worse. Really mean and angry. Then he suffered a complete breakdown and went away for about a year or so to get healthy and recover."

"Oh wow. Why didn't you tell me this before?" I asked.

"I thought I did. Sorry. But anyway, while Dan was gone, I would spend a lot of time with Lisa, to keep her company, you know, and the walls between the apartment and the original part of the house would always be so cold there'd be ice on them, even though the furnace was working well."

"That's strange. So what happened when Dan came home?"

"Well, he seemed to be a lot better, but he would still have really aggressive outbursts and became really verbally abusive towards Lisa. But they continued with the work on the house. After about six months, Lisa couldn't take it anymore and threw Dan out of the house."

"So, Lisa stayed in the apartment then?" I asked.

"Yes, but this is when things really got weird."

"Weird how?"

"Well, when Lisa and Dan moved into the apartment they bought all new appliances—new stove, refrigerator, dishwasher, and microwave. Lisa would go to the grocery store and buy food, and all the food would go bad within a day or so. It was like the food had been left out of the refrigerator," Susan said.

"Did Lisa have the refrigerator checked?"

"Yes, she had the servicemen out there several times, but they couldn't find anything wrong. Lisa would buy chicken and the next day when she went to cook it, it was spoiled by the time she took it out of the refrigerator." Susan shook her head in puzzlement.

"Hmmm. Did anything else happen?"

"Lisa told me that a lot of times she would open the refrigerator and find that all the jars of pickles, mayonnaise, and everything else were opened and dumped inside the refrigerator. Lisa was living alone, Alexis, there was no reason this was happening." Susan looked at me.

"Wow, I wish you'd told me this years ago," I said.

"I really thought I had. I'm sorry."

"No problem. It just confirms it was a demon in that house," I told her.

"How?" Susan asked.

"Well, Dan's drastic change in behavior and his eventual breakdown is, in my opinion, the work of the demon. You said that after he returned to the house his behavior didn't change and his behavior was completely uncharacteristic of how it was before they bought the house, right?"

"Well, yes. So do you think Dan was possessed?" Susan asked.

"I wouldn't go as far to say he was possessed, but I would say he was being controlled by the demon. There's a difference. Possession is when a demon actually enters the body and takes it over. When a person is being controlled by a demon, the demon is practicing a very elevated type of psychological warfare. The demon will put thoughts into someone's head and make them believe they are their own thoughts," I answered.

"Demons can do that?" Susan said, a shocked look on her face.

"Yes," I set down my coffee cup. "Demons are more than capable of crawling into someone's head and wreaking the type of havoc Dan's behavior exemplifies. Besides, Dan probably would have been conceived as a threat to the demon."

"How?" Susan asked, her eyes wide.

"Well, Dan was the one doing most of the work on the house. Perhaps Amon was trying to keep Dan away from his nest in the basement. Amon was protecting his territory in the only way he knew how. Obviously, the incident when Dan and Bob were trying to fix the furnace didn't work, so Amon had to elevate his attack," I answered.

"So what about the stuff that happened to Lisa, the rotting food and all?" Susan asked.

"It could be the work of a poltergeist, but I really think it was the demon."

"Why do you think that?"

"Because a ghost or spirit won't acknowledge places that weren't there when they were alive. Remember how the ghosts wouldn't go into the addition?" I said.

Susan nodded.

"Well, because a demon was never alive like we are, they don't have any emotional attachment to the house and would adapt to any changes made to the house without any problem."

"Is that why some ghost hunters think poltergeists are demons?" Susan asked.

"Yes, poltergeists don't seem to have any emotional attachment to the places they haunt either, but given everything else that's happened, my best guess is that the demon was trying to drive Lisa from the house or scare her into submission so he could control her the way he got control of Dan."

"Makes sense," Susan agreed.

"Lisa's probably lucky she got out of that house when she did." I peered at Susan over the rim of my coffee cup.

"Lord knows what could have happened to her," Susan said, nodding.

As I stated, this conversation took place several years after my experience at the Matthews house. If I'd known then what I know now, the outcome of this story may have been entirely different.

CHAPTER SIX

The morning after Susan and I went to the Matthews house
for the first time, we met at the cemetery down the street
from the house. To my surprise, it was the same cemetery I'd
passed on the way to Susan's the first time.

A stately wrought-iron fence wrapped around the entire
cemetery. I can never decide if the fences around cemeteries are to keep the living out, or the dead inside. It was no
different with this cemetery, although judging from the
energy flowing through the open gate attached to two granite columns on either side of the driveway, I was pretty sure
in this case, at least, the fence was to keep the dead inside. It
failed miserably.

The energy of multiple spirits spilled out of the cemetery gates like a river overflowing its banks. It's unusual
for a cemetery to be haunted, because the people who are
buried there didn't have strong ties to a cemetery when they
were alive. So the presence of so many spirits in one place
felt overwhelming to me.

Because there were so many spirits present, it was impossible for me to adjust my energy to match their vibrations or frequencies. It felt like being in a room full of people.

The only thing to do in that situation is to ignore the weaker spirit energy and just let the strongest energy come through. I've found through experience that the strongest energy normally has the most important message or need.

Susan passed through the gate and stopped about twenty feet away from the entrance. I parked my Jeep behind hers and noticed an unusual grave to my right with a massive pine tree next to it whose branches draped over the grave as if protecting it from the elements. It had a rounded marble headstone and rounded marble slabs surrounding the grave, giving it the appearance of a bed.

"That's Mary Elizabeth's grave," Susan said, following my line of sight.

"It's beautiful," I murmured as I walked towards the grave to get a closer look. When I got closer, I saw that Jacob and his wife were buried next to her with very simple headstones that just had their initials on the top.

Behind Jacob's headstone stood a very tall obelisk that had Jacob's name, date of birth, and date of death, Jacob's wife's name with just years of birth and death, and an elaborate side with Mary Elizabeth's name, her husband's name, the name of her parents, and her date of death.

As much as I tried to concentrate on the Matthews family gravesites, the energy from the remainder of the cemetery commanded my attention.

"I'm going to walk around for a few minutes," I told Susan.

"Okay, I need to clean up Mary Elizabeth's grave anyway," Susan replied, as she kneeled down by the grave and started to pull weeds and clean out the pine needles.

I walked back into the center of the main road and looked around. A small, white wooden building with a wraparound porch with simple wood-plank benches sat in front of me. The road circled around the building on either side and wove to the back of the cemetery.

At the main entrance, a road ran to the left and right and circled the entire cemetery, weaving its way in and out of the massive pine and oak trees that kept the entire graveyard bathed in shade. Rays of sunshine filtered through the branches, illuminating some of the tombstones and making the flecks of granite sparkle like diamonds.

Squirrels scampered across the ground and up the trees, and I could hear their sharp claws grip the bark. Birds were heralding the beautiful fall morning by singing their cheerful songs. Yet something in the cemetery felt entirely off to me.

As I wandered through the graveyard, I'd see something move out of the corner of my eye, but every time I turned around, nothing was there.

After about twenty minutes I wasn't able to track down the source of the bizarre energy I kept feeling, so I joined Susan back at the Matthews gravesite.

"Feel anything?" Susan asked.

"Yeah, but nothing I could put my finger on," I sighed.

I walked around the Matthews family obelisk, reading all the inscriptions.

"Hey, Susan," I said, looking back towards Mary Elizabeth's tombstone.

"What?" Susan asked.

"The energy around the graves feels dark. It's like a dark cloud is hanging over the entire Matthews family grave plot," I told her.

"I wonder why?"

"I don't know, but this whole cemetery is just creepy and it's broad daylight." I crossed my arms around my chest.

"I'm ready to go anyway." Susan stood up by Mary Elizabeth's grave and brushed the dirt off her hands. "Let's come back tonight."

"Okay. I want to go by city hall and see if we can get a map of this place," I said.

We got back into our cars and headed to city hall. After requesting a map of the cemetery, the clerk showed us into a small conference room with a long table and brought in a huge folded map. We thanked her and carefully unfolded the map.

"What the hell?" I pointed to a section of the map.

"What?" Susan asked as she walked over to the part of the massive map I was examining.

"Look," I said, pointing to a section of the cemetery on the map. "There's a Potter's Field in the cemetery."

"That's impossible," Susan said. "There's no open area in that section of the graveyard."

"Let's get a copy of this map and head back to the cemetery," I said.

We took the map out to the clerk and requested two copies. We also asked the clerk if we could see the records on the cemetery.

When we looked at the book of burials, we discovered that the earliest grave listed in the book was 1945. We also noticed a map taped to the inside of the book, and that map didn't have a Potter's Field on it. While the clerk was reluctant to make copies of the large map, she really didn't have a choice.

We knew that there were graves much earlier than that and when we asked the clerk about the earlier records, she told us that the earlier records were at the Historical Society.

"That's a lie," Susan whispered as we walked out of city hall with our copies of the map.

"How do you know?" I asked.

"Because I already asked the Historical Society to see the early records of the cemetery and they told me they didn't have them," Susan said.

"That's interesting. Why would they lie?"

"Because I told you, this town is hiding a secret," Susan said.

As I drove back to the cemetery I wondered if the strange energy I'd felt when we'd been there earlier could have been the spirits of the people buried in Potter's Field trying to get my attention.

I followed Susan through the gates, and we slowly drove past the white building and stopped midway between the building and the back of the cemetery.

We got out of the car and looked at the map so we could identify the people buried around Potter's Field; that would tell us exactly where it was. After a bit of searching, Susan and I found the area of the cemetery marked on our map as Potter's Field.

"There's no open space here," Susan said as she surveyed the rows of tombstones that sat where Potter's Field should have been.

"I know," I said, perplexed. "Let's look at all these graves and see what years the people were buried in."

Susan and I walked up and down the rows calling out years of death; most of the people buried where Potter's Field sat died in the middle 1930s.

"The city must have sold off these gravesites," I said.

"So they buried people on top of the people buried in Potter's Field," Susan said incredulously.

"Looks that way," I shrugged.

"Maybe that's the dirty little secret this town's been hiding," Susan said.

"Could be," I said. "It could also explain why the early records of the cemetery have conveniently disappeared."

"I didn't even think of that," Susan said, her eyes narrowing. "We've got to find those records."

Susan and I walked back to our cars and as I followed her through the cemetery she stopped her car at the Matthews's gravesite.

As I got out of my car and walked towards the graves, I picked up on the presence of Mary Elizabeth.

"She's here," I said.

"Mary Elizabeth?"

"Yes." Then I said to the spirit, "Mary Elizabeth, did you need something?"

As I stood there next to Susan, I saw a vague outline of a woman appear by Mary Elizabeth's grave.

"Do you see her?" I said, grabbing Susan's arm.

"No," Susan replied, peering intently at Mary Elizabeth's grave. "I see kind of a mist. Is that her?"

"Kind of," I answered.

Within a couple of seconds, Mary Elizabeth's image appeared clearer to me, but not to Susan, who could only see a shadowy mist by the grave.

Mary Elizabeth spoke to me, pointing to an empty space of land next to her mother. "Something's missing here."

"What's missing?" I asked.

Mary Elizabeth just kept pointing and repeating the same words until she disappeared.

"What did she say?" Susan asked.

I told Susan what Mary Elizabeth said and we spread out the map of the cemetery over the hood of my truck and looked up the graves of the Matthews family.

"There's no one else listed as buried where Mary Elizabeth was pointing," I said.

"Let's head into town and go by the library; maybe we can find something there," Susan suggested.

We got back into our cars, drove the short distance into town, and raced into the library. We spoke to the librarian, and she gave us a typed oral history by the old caretaker to the cemetery.

In the oral history we read how the caretaker was given twice the amount of money he normally was paid to dig up Jacob's parents' graves in the middle of the night. Jacob's sister, Bella, had been granted a court order to have her parents' graves exhumed and moved.

The oral report stated that when they pulled the caskets out of the ground, the lids came off. Jacob's father was very well preserved and looked like he'd just been buried, while Jacob's mother was just a bag of bones.

The caskets were resealed and then encased in tin before being sent on a train to a town on the other side of the state where Bella lived.

"Why all the mystery?" I asked, after we'd finished reading. "If there was a court order, why dig them up in the middle of the night?"

"I don't know," Susan agreed, shaking her head. "But they died before Mary Elizabeth, so she would know where her grandparents were buried. The whole thing just feels wrong."

I nodded in agreement, and, after making a copy of the pertinent pages in the caretaker's oral history, we left the library and agreed to meet back at the cemetery later that evening to take pictures.

On my way home from the library I stopped by the cemetery and told Mary Elizabeth what Susan and I had found out about her grandparents being moved to a different cemetery and why. She thanked me and disappeared.

There was no reason for me to stay at the cemetery, yet I found myself wandering around among the gravestones. I've always felt most comfortable among the dead—more than the living. The living make me nervous and edgy. Being among the dead calms me down and my greatest moments of peace are in cemeteries.

As I walked through the graveyard I acknowledged various spirits that came forward to greet me, and I knew there was a spirit there I was supposed to talk to for some unknown reason, I just couldn't find it—or they couldn't find me.

You're trying too hard. I silently admonished myself. *Just pick a place and stay there so whoever you're supposed to talk to can find you.*

I walked up the road that ran through the center of the cemetery and settled myself on the bench at the white building to wait. I could see most of the cemetery from my vantage point, including the Matthews family plot.

In a matter of just a few minutes I felt the energy of a spirit approaching me, and the air around me became quite cold.

"Who's there?" I asked aloud.

"It's me. Mary Elizabeth," a soft female voice answered telepathically. "I need to tell you something."

"I'm listening," I said.

"There's something in my house—something bad. I don't know what it is, but it scares me. Promise me you'll be careful," Mary Elizabeth pleaded.

"I promise," I said. "Where in the house is this spirit, Mary Elizabeth?"

"In the basement. It's the room to the left when you come down the staircase," she answered.

Before I could respond, I felt Mary Elizabeth's energy become weak and start to fade and I could feel the spirit of Mary Elizabeth move off into the distance. Reluctantly, I got up from the bench and walked back to my car.

That night I told my husband I was meeting Susan for coffee and headed out of the house around ten-thirty. I pulled into the cemetery to find Susan already snapping pictures with her digital camera.

While she was busy with that, I wandered through the large cemetery to get a feel for the different energies. After about a half hour I couldn't really track anything down, so I sat down on the bench that wrapped around three sides of the white building. I saw the flash from Susan's camera illuminating part of the cemetery every time she squeezed off another shot.

To be honest, I really wasn't paying attention to my surroundings because I was still digesting the information we'd found out earlier in the day regarding the late-night exhumation of Jacob's parents' graves.

In fact, I was so lost in thought that I almost jumped out of my skin when Susan came up and sat down next to me on the bench.

"Sorry," Susan laughed.

"It's okay," I said, looking around the cemetery that was illuminated by the light of the moon in the clear fall sky. "What the....?"

"What?" Susan said.

"Just sit quietly and look around the cemetery," I told her. "Look closely and you'll see shadows of what look like people darting around the trees. The shadows are too big to be animals."

Susan and I sat and gazed out at the cemetery; every couple of minutes we saw a shadow of what looked like a person dart out from one of the trees only to disappear behind another tree.

"Could there be other people in here?" I whispered.

"No," Susan said. "No other cars have come in since we've been here, and the shadows are moving way too fast to be people."

"You're right," I said, watching another shadow dart behind a tall tombstone. "We're being surrounded."

"Maybe we should go," Susan looked around nervously.

"Yeah. Not a bad idea," I said, rising from the bench.

"Let's drop your car off at my house and take my car. There are a few more places I want to check out," Susan suggested.

We drove to Susan's house and I parked my truck in her driveway. We drove to the Matthews house and Susan took a few pictures. As we left the house, we drove back towards the cemetery.

"Alexis. There's a car that came out of nowhere and it's right on my ass," Susan exclaimed.

I looked out the back window and saw the headlights of a car right on the bumper of Susan's truck.

"What's up with that?" I said.

"I don't know," Susan said as she tapped her brakes and eased her Jeep onto the shoulder of the road to let the car pass.

The car raced past us and, just as Susan was getting back on the road, I noticed it was a late-model dark-colored Pontiac. The left back taillight was busted out and the white of the taillight shone brightly in the darkness. The car turned around and came back at us from the opposite direction.

"Hang on!" Susan yelled as she slammed on the brakes and turned her Jeep onto a side street. She floored the truck and we raced down the road until we came to a vacant house that had just been built behind the cemetery. Susan pulled into the driveway and cut the lights to her Jeep. We ducked down in the seat and saw the car that had been following us race past and down the road.

Once their taillights disappeared, Susan started up the Jeep and we went in the opposite direction.

"Who the hell was that?" I asked.

"I don't know," Susan said. "But whoever it was probably doesn't like that we're poking around asking questions in town."

"You're probably right. Looks like we've struck a nerve somewhere," I chuckled.

"Good," Susan laughed evilly. "Looks like us crazy old bitches have stirred the cauldron. Let's just wait and see what floats to the top."

The next day Susan and I went into town to talk to Fred, the president of the Historical Society, about the Potter's Field in the town cemetery.

Fred looked at the map and scratched his head. "I didn't even know there was a Potter's Field in the cemetery."

"Really?" I said in disbelief.

"No, really. This is all news to me," Fred said. "It's interesting, though, for sure."

"Are you sure the Historical Society doesn't have the records for the cemetery that go back to when it was first established?" Susan asked.

"I'm sure. After you asked me a few months back I double-checked. We don't have them. They must be at city hall, or it's possible they were lost over the years."

"Thanks for your help," Susan and I said as we got up to leave. Neither one of us exactly bought Fred's story, but we didn't have any proof to the contrary.

As we walked down Main Street towards our trucks, Susan grabbed my arm.

"Will you look at that?" She pointed towards the police station.

I saw that she was pointing at a late-model Pontiac sitting in a parking place reserved for police cars.

"You don't think that's the same car that followed us last night, do you?" I said.

"Let's find out," Susan answered.

We walked down the sidewalk past the car and then turned around and looked at the rear taillights of the vehicle. We noticed that the left taillight was broken, exposing the lightbulb—just like the one that had come after us the night before.

"I wonder who the car belongs to?" I asked.

"I don't know, but I'm sure as hell going to find out," Susan said. "I know one of the policemen. I'll ask him." Susan looked at her watch. "I need to get home. I'll catch you later."

Susan and I bid each other goodbye and, while she headed home, I decided to go into the antique store located next to the Historical Society.

The store was run by two older women who'd been around this area almost their entire lives. Several times a week some of the women from town would gather in the store to have coffee and baked goods and to exchange local gossip. I hoped this was one of those mornings.

As I walked into the store I was greeted by the smell of lemon furniture polish, fresh coffee, and cinnamon rolls. Two women sat in antique chairs sipping their coffee and talking.

Agnes, the woman who owned the store, recognized me because I'd purchased several pieces of furniture from the store when we moved into our house.

"Alexis! I haven't seen you in a long time. Grab some coffee and a roll and sit down," Agnes said, greeting me warmly. She introduced me to Rebecca and Sarah and, with a cup of coffee in hand, I found myself a spot in a comfy overstuffed chair.

"You know, Martha at the library told me there have been two women digging around for information on the Matthews family," Rebecca said.

I almost choked on my cinnamon roll, but recovered nicely and remained quiet—and attentive.

"Really?" Sarah asked.

"Yes, they've been nosing around city hall asking for records of the cemetery too," Agnes said. "Fred over at the Historical Society mentioned something to me just a little bit ago about it."

"Those women should be careful. There're folks in this town that aren't going to take too kindly to having the past dredged up. They should just let sleeping dogs lie," Rebecca responded.

"Why is that?" I asked. "I'm sorry, but I'm new in town and am just curious."

"It's because of the Matthews house. You know the one up the road a bit, that big empty mansion," Agnes said.

"Yes. I know the house," I answered.

"Well," Sarah said, leaning forward in her chair, "that house is haunted. I think some of the old timers in town are afraid that if someone goes poking around where they don't belong, the ghosts will get angry and take out their revenge on the whole town."

"Seriously?" I asked.

"Yes. The Matthews family, from what I've heard, were very private and very powerful around these parts a long time ago. Some people say the ghost of old Jacob still roams the house," Sarah answered.

"So what if he does?" I said. "I'm not trying to be difficult, really. But I thought people around here liked the ghosts. I mean I went on the candlelight walk a few months ago and everyone on the walk seemed fascinated by the ghost stories, even more than the history."

"Oh, people around here are fascinated by the ghosts, but they're also very superstitious and afraid of them. In my opinion, whoever is poking their noses in where they don't belong are asking for nothing but trouble—not just from the ghosts, but from some of the people in town," Agnes said.

"Why? What are people around here afraid those women are going to find out? It can't just be because of the ghosts," I said.

Rebecca shifted uncomfortably in her chair before getting up to pour more coffee. "This town has a bit of a sordid past, a past that I'm sure a lot of people in town might not be proud of, because in most cases it involves their parents or grandparents. It would be best if those women just left things be. No point picking the scab off the wound," Rebecca stated.

"I'm sure you're right," I said. "You don't think those women are in any real danger, do you?"

"Oh, I don't think anyone would hurt them," Sarah said, setting her coffee cup down hard on the table next to her. "But I do think some people in town would try to put a good scare into them to get them to stop poking their noses in where they don't belong. I heard someone was in the cemetery taking pictures last night. It was probably them."

"Why would anyone take pictures at night in a cemetery?" Agnes clucked. "What could they be looking for?"

"Ghosts," I answered. "Some ghost hunters take pictures at night in cemeteries because they believe the energy from the flash of their camera will illuminate any spirits that are there."

"Really?" Rebecca said.

"Yes. It's a common belief among a lot of people that ghosts are made up of energy. The flash on a camera is also a form of energy. Energy reacts to energy."

"How do you know so much about all this?" Sarah asked suspiciously.

"I watch all those ghost shows on television," I answered. It was the truth, but not the whole truth. Given the hostility of the women, I didn't want to tell them I was one of the women they were talking about.

"Well, it just all seems strange to me. Those women are doing nothing except asking for trouble," Rebecca said. The other women nodded in agreement.

A customer walked into the store, which, luckily for me, stalled the conversation, and the women turned to talking about their families while Agnes waited on her customer.

I sat back in my chair and thought about what the women told me. A few minutes later I made an excuse about having housework to do and left.

On my way home I decided to stop by city hall and talk to one of the clerks about the early records for the cemetery. This time I was helped by a tiny older woman who introduced herself as Sharon.

I told her that I was doing genealogy research and wondered if the city had the records for the cemetery. She pointed out the book Susan and I'd looked at before, and I explained to her that I wanted the records before 1945.

She thought for a moment, then excused herself and disappeared into a back room. She emerged a few minutes later with a stack of laminated papers and handed them to me; they were the old records for the cemetery!

"Interesting," I told her. "When I was in here a few days ago I was told your office didn't have the records."

"Some of the people here just don't know where to look," she told me with a wink. "I found them in a box in the vault. I secretly hide stuff like this so it doesn't mysteriously disappear."

"Do things tend to disappear around here?" I asked her.

"Between you and me," she whispered, leaning over the counter, "there are certain things people just want to sweep under the carpet in this town. Once I figured out we were missing some documents, I started to hide stuff. I've worked here twenty-five years. I've got quite a stash."

"What documents are missing?" I whispered.

"Stupid stuff no one would even care about. I know some old city records have disappeared, but I just knew we had them and now we don't. I wish I'd taken the time to read them now," Sharon said.

"Why would someone steal those records?"

"I wish I knew. I've lived here all my life and I still can't figure out what the big deal is. I must be missing something somewhere," Sharon sighed.

"Do you have anything in your secret stash about the Matthews family?" I asked.

"No, *that* I know for sure. You're not the first person to be asking about that family. Some of their descendants that live on the other side of the state were in here a while back asking that same question."

"I see. Could I please get two copies of these old cemetery records? I'll pay for the copies," I said.

"Of course. If you want to wait for a little bit I can do it now. We're not real busy today," Sharon offered. "Don't blame you for not wanting to leave without these records. You never know if they'll disappear too."

"That would be great. Thanks."

A little while later Sharon reappeared from a back room and handed me two copies of the cemetery records. I paid her and thanked her profusely before heading home.

I spent the better part of the afternoon poring over the records and I discovered that it gave names, when available, of the people buried in Potter's Field, but didn't yield any information other than what I already knew about the Matthews family.

CHAPTER SEVEN

Early the next morning, Susan called and asked if I wanted to meet her for lunch; I readily agreed.

Around noon I pulled into the local diner and found Susan waiting for me at a back booth. She had a notebook with her, and had already ordered herself a coffee and me a Diet Coke.

"Hey, how's it going?" I slid into the seat across from her.

"Good. What's up with you? You look like the cat that swallowed the canary," Susan laughed.

"Interesting how things just kind of show up around here, isn't it?" I said with a wry grin as I handed her a copy of the cemetery records.

"Where did you find these?" Susan asked, eagerly leafing through the records.

I told Susan about the conversations I'd had with the women in the antique store and at the clerk's office.

"Wow, the people in this town sure are paranoid about something," Susan said.

"I agree, but I'm not convinced that selling the plots over Potter's Field is the big secret," I shrugged.

"It could be," Susan said, as she looked back through the records.

"Why do you say that?" I asked.

"Well, look at some of the dates the people were buried in Potter's Field. There are dates from the 1850s to the 1890s," Susan said.

"Okay. So?"

"So, the city sold off those grave plots in the 1930s. There's a law that says you can't disturb a grave that's less than a hundred years old without obtaining the heir's permission. Technically, because these people were buried in Potter's Field, that law may not apply because the expense of the burial was absorbed by the city, but I'd bet you just about anything that they sold off the gravesites where Potter's Field was without notifying any of the heirs and giving them first dibs on those grave plots," Susan speculated.

"You're probably right," I shrugged. "But would that be enough to steal records and have the police follow us?"

"Look at the facts. The police didn't start following us until we started asking questions about the cemetery," Susan pointed out. "And don't think for a second those women at the antique store didn't know who you were. That whole conversation, in my opinion, was nothing more than veiled warnings."

"I agree with you about why the police were following us, but I'm not convinced the women in the antique store were warning me about anything," I said. "We can't assume anything. It's all just speculation at this point."

"Maybe I am being a little paranoid."

"You think?" I laughed.

"Did the records say anything interesting about Mary Elizabeth?" Susan asked.

"Yeah, get this. Mary Elizabeth, according to these records, is listed as Mary Elizabeth Gibbons—not Matthews, and not by her married name. But, there is a woman named Mary Elizabeth Gibbons buried in the cemetery a few rows over."

"Really? How could anyone make that mistake, especially with such an influential family like the Matthews?"

"You're assuming it was a mistake," I answered. "But what if it wasn't? It's like no one wanted to acknowledge the existence of Mary Elizabeth anywhere. I've checked some of the other records against the map we have of the cemetery, and there are no other errors that I've found so far."

"That's strange. Thank goodness Mary Elizabeth's name is on the headstone and the Matthews monument, or she wouldn't even be a footnote in the history of this place," Susan said.

"It's really very sad, you know?"

"It is," Susan agreed. "You're not the only one who had a productive afternoon yesterday. Get this, I found out that the car that followed us the other night is an undercover police car, and I spent this morning in town and found out some stuff." Susan eyes were gleaming as she spoke.

"Awesome," I paused as the waitress refilled our drinks. When she left the table, I asked Susan, "What did you find out?"

"Well," Susan leaned across the table in a conspiratorial manner, "I found out that Jacob died a few days after he took a terrible fall down the stairs in his wheelchair."

"Really? Now that's interesting," I said, digesting this new piece of information as I sipped my Diet Coke.

"Yeah, I thought so too. So what if Jacob got pushed down the stairs and it wasn't an accident?" Susan asked.

"It's a possibility, but we have no proof. It's pure speculation," I said.

"True, but it's something to think about," Susan raised an eyebrow.

"It is." We stopped talking as the waitress delivered our lunch, then I asked, "What else did you find out?"

"Well, when I was talking to my friend in the police department about that car that followed us, he told me that they are getting calls weekly from the neighbors because some kids or a group of people are breaking into the Matthews house to see if they can find the ghosts. He said they've found people in the house sitting in a circle of candles either chanting or trying to communicate with whatever ghosts haunt the place," Susan said, munching on an onion ring.

"No wonder one of the ghosts tries to push people down the stairs!" I laughed. "I'd be pissed off too."

"Exactly," Susan agreed. "But you know what's so weird?"

"What?"

"I've been trying to find out information about this family for the last five years, and there's virtually no paper trail. Other than Robert and Jacob's probate records, there's really not much else. I can't even find a birth certificate, marriage certificate, or death certificate for Mary Elizabeth. I've checked everywhere. And now her name is listed wrong in the cemetery records." Susan shook her head sadly.

"That's a shame," I said.

"It is. I did find a newspaper article in the library this morning that stated when Jacob died no one really mourned his death. If I remember correctly, Fred told us after the candlelight walk that Jacob Matthews was rather bad tempered, a ruthless business man, and not well liked by people in town," Susan stated.

"Yes, I remember him saying something about that. So, what about it?"

"Well, I found an article a few months ago that said when Jacob's father Robert died, he left a lot of money to the town to build a school. Jacob fought giving the money to the city and took the case all the way to the state supreme court. He lost, of course, but it says a lot about his character," Susan said.

"Yes, it does. Sounds like he was kind of greedy to me," I concurred.

"So wouldn't it make sense that Jacob would be the ghost on the third floor of the house, protecting his property and the family secrets?" Susan asked.

"It does make sense. Plus there's that picture we took that has the old-fashioned wheelchair in it. It could be him verifying his identity."

"I think so too," Susan said. "Do you think you can get Jacob to talk to you?"

"I don't know. It's worth a shot," I said.

"Let's go there after lunch and find out," Susan suggested, and I agreed.

"So, to change the subject, tell me more about Dan and Lisa," I said.

"Well, Dan has lived here most his life. Lisa moved here about ten years ago. I met Lisa when I worked at the yarn store in town. We became friends and Bob and Dan hit it off real well."

"How long have they owned the Matthews house?"

"About five years. Although now that they're divorced and Lisa's remarried, I'm not sure what they're going to do with the house."

"I wish I could buy it and restore it," I said wistfully.

"Me too," Susan agreed.

Susan and I paid our bills and headed over to the Matthews house. On the way over, I thought about all the paranormal activity that had been reported about the house and what I'd experienced up to that point.

My years as a ghost hunter had taught me that, based on the events the current owners had experienced, whatever we were dealing with didn't want anyone there; yet I'd felt very welcomed in the home by the spirits that resided there, with the exception of the room in the basement.

Or could it have been the spirits didn't want certain people there? Susan's research told us that Jacob was a rather mean man and we assumed Jacob was the one responsible for the majority of activity in the house in order to chase out the living and protect the long-forgotten secrets of the Matthews family, such as what really happened to Mary Elizabeth, and countless other secrets Susan and I probably weren't even aware of.

But the entity in the basement was an entirely different story. I really wasn't sure exactly what Susan and I were dealing with and that bothered me. Not knowing what type of entity we were dealing with made it difficult to know how hard I could push the phantom to reveal his identity and his motives.

I made a mental note to revisit the room in the basement and *not* run away in fear again. Having never come up against an entity as powerful as this one, I wasn't quite sure what I was going to do to protect myself and stand up to this negative force, but I decided to play it by ear and figure it out as I went.

CHAPTER EIGHT

Susan and I pulled into the driveway of the Matthews house. As soon as I stepped out of the car I noticed that the energy of the house had changed from when I was there the first time. The energy around the house felt charged with a sense of anticipation, almost as if it was awaiting our return.

I let myself absorb that wave of energy and opened myself up to feel more: I wanted to know everything about this house. Then I felt something that made me stop in my tracks.

"It knows," I whispered to Susan.

"What knows?" Susan asked, giving me a sideways glance.

"The house. It knows," I said in a more normal tone of voice.

"Knows what?"

"That we know what's happened here. I can't explain it, but the house is waiting for something, someone. It's preparing to defend itself," I answered.

"Against what?" Susan said.

"Us," I whispered.

"It's afraid we're going to learn the truth," Susan stated matter-of-factly. "Let's go."

I nodded in agreement and followed Susan through the door to the apartment and we immediately made our way into the original section of the house. We padded down the hallway towards the staircase and headed up to the second floor.

When we reached the second floor, I attempted to make contact with a young woman. Susan and I felt a kind, gentle, feminine presence around us and assumed that Mary Elizabeth had joined us.

I closed my eyes and took a few deep breaths so I could adjust my energy vibrations to match Mary Elizabeth's.

"Mary Elizabeth," I said. "We mean you no harm and we're not here to make you leave. We just want to know your story."

"Hello. I'm so glad you came back." Mary Elizabeth spoke with me telepathically. Her voice sounded like it was coming out of a fog. Distant, but clear enough to understand.

"We're glad to be back," I told her.

"Can you help my father?" Mary Elizabeth asked.

"Help your father do what?" I replied.

"Help him leave this place and join Mother and me," Mary Elizabeth said.

"So you've crossed over?" I thought she had, but wanted confirmation.

"Yes. I come back to visit my father."

"Mary Elizabeth, I can't make your father leave, but I will talk to him," I promised. "Your father, he's on the third floor, right?"

"Yes. He really likes when you and your friend come to visit. He gets so lonely. Thank you for trying to help him," she said.

"Mary Elizabeth, can you tell us what happened to you? How you died?" I asked.

"I can show you," Mary Elizabeth said.

As Mary Elizabeth talked to me through telepathy, she also transmitted pictures into my head of the argument taking place on the second-floor landing between herself and a man, although I couldn't make out who the man was. I saw the argument become heated and the man grabbed her arm. When she jerked away, she lost her balance and fell down the stairs, breaking her neck.

It's a little difficult to explain how a spirit shows me pictures or clips of their lives, although I have a couple of theories of how this is possible. One theory is that they do it through telepathy, and the second is that can project the image they want me to see using energy, and my brain is able to interpret that energy in some way. In my mind I either see photographs or a movie, depending on how the spirit projected the information to me.

I thanked Mary Elizabeth for showing me the image, then asked, "Who were you arguing with, Mary Elizabeth?"

"It doesn't matter. It was an accident," she said. "I must take leave of you now. Have a pleasant afternoon." With those words she was gone.

Susan was standing next to me, impatiently squirming around like a small child."What did she tell you?" Susan asked.

I told Susan what I saw and what Mary Elizabeth had told me, and that we had confirmation that Jacob was the spirit on the third floor—well, as much confirmation as we could get.

As soon as we reached the third-floor landing, I felt the spirit surround me; it felt almost smothering—kind of like a ghost's way of giving a bear hug. Susan started taking pictures and was able to confirm that, because of the white ectoplasmic mist around me, Jacob was indeed present.

Susan and I both greeted him and once again started to play the twenty-questions game. However, it became quite apparent that, because of the lack of response, Jacob didn't want to play; it was more than likely he just wanted company.

We tried in vain to coax him to tell us how Mary Elizabeth died, or to confirm that we were, in fact, talking to Jacob. We knew through several old newspaper articles that Jacob wasn't confined to a wheelchair at the time of Mary Elizabeth's death, but all attempts to communicate with him about Mary Elizabeth were met with silence.

The fact that Jacob didn't want to communicate was not unusual. As a medium, I can find the ghost, but I can't force the ghost to talk to me. They have to choose to communicate. Kind of like the old adage, "You can lead a horse to water, but you can't make him drink."

"Okay, Jacob. I get you don't want to talk about how Mary Elizabeth died, so let's change the subject, shall we?"

I said. "Why won't you go and join Mary Elizabeth and your wife? Aren't you lonely?"

"I get so lonely," Jacob admitted to me, his soft, thready voice filled with sadness. "But if I go, I'm going to be judged for those things I did in life. I was a real bastard. I will be sent to hell, and not be with my family. At least here, in this house, I get to see my daughter occasionally."

"I understand, Jacob." I'd run across this type of spirit before. They don't want to cross to the other side because of what their religion has taught them about judgment day. It's hard to convince them otherwise, and I debated with myself whether it was worth it or not to have that discussion with Jacob. I decided against it because right then he was my only source of information and his defensive energy was telling me it would be an exercise in futility.

After about a half hour of Jacob only showing me pictures of how the house used to look when he lived there but nothing about Mary Elizabeth, we decided to give it up and head down to the basement. I wanted another crack at that room.

We crept down the basement stairs, and Susan wandered off at my request to take some more pictures. I honestly wasn't sure what the entity in that room was, and I didn't want to put Susan in any danger.

Once I was sure Susan was safely on the other side of the basement, I cautiously walked into the room with the dirt floor. My heart was pounding so hard it felt like it was going to burst out of my chest. I took a few deep breaths to slow it down, as a fast heartbeat could be construed as fear by a ghost or spirit. It wouldn't have been too far from the truth. I was scared.

Pushing the fear aside and calming myself, I walked into the center of the room and braced myself for the onslaught of energy I'd felt before. The first wave hit me hard, but I held my ground and let it flow through me.

I became keenly aware of a particularly menacing presence at the other end of the room. My head began to ache terribly and I became nauseated. Instinctively, I knew I should get out of there, but I stayed put.

Ghost hunting has taught me that fear is the enemy when facing an entity, and with some types of ghosts or spirits, fear actually makes them stronger and more powerful. There wasn't anything in the world that would get me out of that room now.

I opened myself up psychically as much as I dared, trying to get a feeling for the phantom across the room from me, but it stayed just outside of my radar. Whoever it was didn't want me to learn anything about them, at least not yet.

In reality, I couldn't blame the ghost or spirit for being cautious when a stranger approached, but given what happened to Dan and Bob in this very room, caution was the word of the day.

All I could pick up on was that this entity was very powerful and a force to be reckoned with even on a good day. I also got the distinct impression that a body might be buried in the room.

So the question then became if there was a body buried in this room, was this powerful entity protecting it and if so, why? The second question then would be whose body could it be? I also noticed that the energy seemed to be coming from a hole in the far wall that led under the front porch, not the basement itself.

A loud bang came from another part of the basement and jolted me back into the present.

"Susan? Was that you?" I called out.

"No, I thought it was you," Susan joined me at the bottom of the basement stairs.

"You heard that noise, right?" I asked.

"Yeah, a banging noise. I came to see if you were okay," Susan answered.

"I'm pretty sure we're the only ones in the house, but let's go make sure someone didn't come in," I suggested.

We looked around the entire house to see if anything seemed out of place, but found nothing. We locked up the house and decided to go get some coffee.

At the restaurant, I told Susan what I'd felt in the furnace room of the basement, and we started to speculate about who, if anyone, could be buried in either the basement or under the front porch.

"I wonder if it could be Mary Elizabeth's husband, Clinton," Susan said. "I know from my research that Jacob owned a general store and pharmacy at the time of Mary Elizabeth's death. At that time, poisons were readily available over the counter. It would be nothing for Jacob to poison Clinton and bury him in the basement."

"True. But where's the motive?" I asked.

"Well, when I was going through Robert Matthews's probate records I found out that he left Mary Elizabeth, his granddaughter, about twenty thousand dollars. Even by today's standards that's a lot of money. With Mary Elizabeth dead, Clinton stood to inherit a lot of money."

"Maybe. Mary Elizabeth would have been about nine when Robert died, and with Jacob handling her money, it would have grown to a sizeable amount at the time of her death," I surmised.

"Exactly, and given Jacob's purported reputation for being nasty, and the fact that Clinton would have stood to inherit Mary Elizabeth's sizable fortune, it seems plausible. All Jacob would have had to say was that Clinton left town after Mary Elizabeth's death and went to join his family. No one would have questioned it." Susan took a sip of coffee.

"That's true. But remember, there have been a lot of owners of the property and it's possible that it could be someone else, or even a family pet, buried there. The truth is, we can't prove a body is actually buried in the basement or under the porch, and if there is a body, it could be just about anyone, and placed there long before the house was even constructed. I'm not ready to peg anyone as a murderer; it's all just speculation."

"We could talk to Dan and Lisa about digging down there to see." Susan shook her head. "But to be honest, I really don't have the stomach for it and I don't think Dan and Lisa would agree to it anyway."

"Yeah," I sighed. "Besides, some things are better left alone." I remembered the menacing energy I felt in that room in the basement. I wasn't ready to go poking around down there without knowing what type of entity I was dealing with.

Thinking these and other equally unpleasant thoughts, Susan and I parted ways and I headed home to again go over some of the information we'd gathered on the family.

That night, my husband and I joined some friends for dinner at a local restaurant. While having a conversation with our friends, I suddenly felt as if I was floating and, before I knew it, I saw myself coming in for a landing on the third floor of the house on the hill. By this, I mean I literally saw the top of my shoes come closer to the hardwood floor of the house. I was hanging in midair!

I was shocked. Nothing like this had ever happened to me before, and all I knew was that I had to get out of the Matthews house fast. But how? I wasn't even sure how I got there!

After squashing the feeling of panic that ricocheted through me, I realized that maybe I could "think" my way back. In other words, will myself back to where I'd been.

I focused on my husband and friends sitting in the restaurant, and felt myself being pulled backwards at a rapid rate of speed. I literally slammed back into my body, which caused me to visibly jump.

"Alexis! Alexis!" my husband, Kyle, said, his eyes filled with concern.

"What? I'm fine," I said, a bit dazed.

"Are you okay?" my friend Carol asked.

"Yes. Sorry, I was just lost in thought," I lied.

"Are you sure you're okay?" Kyle asked.

"Yes. I need to go to the restroom. I'll be right back," I jumped off the barstool–high chair and walked into the ladies room.

Thank goodness the bathroom was empty when I entered it; I stood at the sink trying to catch my breath and attempted to figure out what the hell had just happened. Realizing I couldn't be gone long for fear of scaring my husband and friends even more, I splashed some cold water on my face and rejoined them at the table.

As I was getting ready for bed that night, Kyle asked, "So, what really happened at the restaurant?"

"Nothing, I was just thinking about something," I said, not daring to look at him.

"It's that house you and Susan have been working on, isn't it?" He narrowed his eyes at me.

"Yes," I sighed. "I just can't seem to get it out of my head."

"You've become obsessed with that house. I don't want you going there anymore."

"Oh, I'm going back," I said defiantly. "And there's nothing you can do to stop me. There's an entity in that place that I can't figure out, and I won't rest until I find out what it is."

"That's what spaced you out at the restaurant?" Kyle asked.

"Something like that," I told him. "I'm tired. I'm going to bed."

Kyle threw his hands up in disgust and walked out of the bedroom.

I felt bad not telling him exactly what had happened, but he wouldn't have understood and I didn't have the strength to try to convince him that what I do is real, that ghosts are real—and that not telling him was the only way I could think of to keep him safe.

I'm still at a loss to explain what happened in the restaurant. As I write this and think about that night, it's entirely possible that I astral traveled back to the house. Astral travel is when a person leaves their physical body and travels to another place. Many people do this unconsciously while they sleep, although with practice, it can be done at will.

Considering I was wide awake when this happened, and have never learned how to consciously astral travel, I'm not convinced this is what happened.

I believe I was pulled back to the Matthews house by an entity. I'm positive that it was the third-floor landing I saw, because I noticed the stairs leading down to the second floor and the wall that enclosed the stairway to the cupola.

I also know what happened would have probably scared another person half to death, and I have to admit, it did shake me up, but it didn't scare me. It only served to make me even more curious about the phantoms that dwelled in the house on the hill.

I have an overwhelming sense of curiosity, and in most cases that curiosity overrides my fear—and my common sense.

CHAPTER NINE

You'd think the incident at the restaurant and my argument with Kyle would have been enough to discourage me from pursuing any further investigation into the house, but it didn't. In fact, it only served to ignite my curiosity even more.

Susan and I plunged headfirst into unmasking the secrets of the Matthews family, and even more importantly, into discovering the identity of the powerful entity in the basement.

My curiosity about the Matthews house and its phantom occupants turned into an obsession. It occupied every waking moment and flashed through my dreams like shadows.

Susan and I were regularly followed by the unmarked police car, but it never became as aggressive as it did the first night it followed us. Then one night, while Susan and I were out taking pictures, a marked police car followed us around for about an hour. It stayed some distance behind us, but close enough that we knew it was there.

A friend of Susan's had told her about a stretch of dirt road that creeped her out, so we decided to drive over there and check it out. We pulled well onto the shoulder of the road and got out of the car so Susan could take some pictures.

The marked police car pulled in about one hundred feet behind us and turned on their overhead red and blue flashing lights.

"Enough is enough! Those policemen and I are going to have us some hell!" I said. "If they don't have the guts to confront us, I'm going to confront them."

"Go for it, you crazy old bitch. I've got bail money," Susan chuckled.

With a determined stride, I walked purposefully towards the police car. As soon as I got within fifty feet of the car, the policemen turned off the flashing lights, backed their car up and turned around fast, sending gravel and dust flying everywhere. The police car raced down the road and out of sight.

"What the hell was that all about?" Susan asked.

"Guess they didn't want to engage in a little friendly conversation," I laughed.

"Or they didn't want to face police harassment charges," Susan giggled.

"That too," I said.

After that night, Susan and I were never followed by the police again, although we still can't figure out why they followed us in the first place.

During the weeks that followed, the gray wolf would show up at my house occasionally but continued to just be more of a benign presence than anything else. I would see the wolf lying under my desk, on the stairway landing, and sometimes riding shotgun in my car. But truthfully, I was much more obsessed with the house and its spirits and really didn't give the wolf much thought. I just acknowledged its presence and continued on with my work.

I spent countless hours communicating with Jacob on the third floor of the house in an attempt to get him to reveal the secrets he'd kept hidden for more than one hundred years. Jacob, however, was not interested in talking about the past; he was more interested in the news of the day and events going on in a world he could no longer be a part of. So almost every day I visited Jacob with my morning newspaper and read it to him. All of this was fun in a way, but got me no closer to finding out what happened to Mary Elizabeth or what other secrets lay hidden in the house.

Mary Elizabeth's spirit didn't frequent the house much, and when she was there she flitted in and out of the second-floor rooms like a moth looking for a place to rest.

While always friendly and playful, she, too, refused to discuss the circumstances surrounding her death. It became painfully obvious that Mary Elizabeth was at peace with her fate, while Susan was fixated on it.

I, on the other hand, became obsessed with the entity that lived in the basement. Every time I entered the house I became aware of its energy. When I asked Jacob about the spirit that lived in the basement, he would become very stern and tell me to stay away from it—that he wasn't sure what it was, but, in his opinion, the creature in the basement had never been alive in human form.

It stayed far enough away from me as to not chase me out of the house, but at the same time, its dark, heavy presence became a constant companion while in the home.

While I hesitate to say it was stalking me, I got the feeling that it was as curious about me as I was about it. While I was aware of its presence, I didn't acknowledge it in any way in hopes it would tire of its little game and leave me alone.

I know now that it was stalking me the way a hunter stalks its prey before going in for the kill. Every time I take the time to stop and think about the game of cat and mouse I unwittingly played with this demon, it sends chills down my spine and makes every hair on my body stand on end.

However, if I knew then what I know now, I would still have gone back to that house—not just in spite of the demon, but because of the demon. My obsession with the beast that lived in the basement of that house was so strong it negated almost everything else going on in my life at that time. So yes, I would do it all over again, but next time I would be a lot smarter in my encounters with the demon.

One day Susan and I got a huge shock: Dan and Lisa put the house up for sale. We were concerned that we would no longer have access to the house once it sold. In fact, the city was calling it a public nuisance and wanted it torn down because of all the kids and strange religious-cult groups breaking into the house.

While upset at the thought of the house changing hands, we felt we'd learned just about everything there was to know about the house itself and could only hope that the new owners would restore the house to its former glory.

The only time I met Dan and Lisa was when I drove by the Matthews house one day on my way into town. Dan and Lisa were having a garage sale in the side yard of the house. I stopped and wandered through the sale, curious as to what they were getting rid of. Most of the items up for sale had been kept in storage in the Matthews house's old garage.

I stood back for a minute or two watching people's reactions to the Matthews house. I noticed many people read the list of items for sale that were inside the house, which was posted on a big piece of poster board. A woman, who I assumed was Lisa, would take someone inside the house, but the person would come out a minute or two later and appeared to not be able to get to their car fast enough and get out of there.

"Curious," I thought.

I looked closer at the poster board and then asked Lisa to take me inside to look at a chair listed for sale.

Lisa led me through the apartment and into the parlor. I immediately felt the energy of the entity in the basement radiating up through the floor, and it was stronger than it'd ever been. *No wonder people are fleeing the house like rats from a sinking ship*, I thought.

"I'm Alexis, Susan's friend," I introduced myself as Lisa pointed out the chair I'd wanted to see.

"I hate this house. It's brought nothing but trouble since the day we bought it. If I were you, I'd stay out of here before it destroys your life too," Lisa stated.

"Why do you say that?" I was taken aback by her abruptness.

"Susan told me you're psychic, right?" Lisa asked.

"Yes."

"Then you figure it out," Lisa said and walked out of room leaving me standing there with my mouth hanging open. Lisa's manner, while not exactly rude, wasn't open and friendly and bordered on hostile. Her energy felt beaten down, oppressed, and bitter.

I stood in the center of the old parlor dumbfounded for a few minutes.

When I went back outside, I looked around to see what other items were for sale. There were many of the original light fixtures, the ceramic molds from the basement, and other household items that obviously came from their homes and not the Matthews house.

I found a painting I liked of a sailboat on the open water and picked it up to purchase. As I was walking around the sale holding the painting, Dan walked up to me and snatched it out of my hand.

"Where did you get this?" he demanded.

"It was over there, leaning against that tree," I told him.

"This is not for sale," he said angrily and stormed off.

As I watched him walk away I noticed that his energy felt heavy and filled with anger, rage, and hate. I concentrated on him and could "see" a dark cloud wrapped around him like a blanket. As I walked back to my car I couldn't help but wonder if my energy felt oppressed like Lisa's did and if a dark cloud was surrounding me. I hated to admit it to myself, but it was sure beginning to feel that way.

A couple of weeks later I received a telephone call from the realtor who listed the Matthews house. She'd been given my number by the Historical Society and was told I was the leading authority on the house and the Matthews family. She asked if I would conduct a tour for the realtors in her office and tell them the history of the house.

She also wanted to conduct the tour at night, despite my telling them there wasn't any electricity or heat in the house and it was the middle of winter. This led me to believe they were more curious about the ghosts than the house, and I reluctantly agreed. However, I was determined to stick with the history of the house and leave the ghosts out of the tour.

On the specified evening, I met the realtor and a group of about thirty-five people at the Matthews house. They were all bundled up in winter jackets and armed with flashlights and cameras.

We wound our way through the cavernous home and I told them what the rooms were once used for, and the history of the Matthews family. I took every precaution not to tell them about the ghosts, the ghost stories, or make any other reference to the phantoms that roamed the rooms and hallways of the once-glorious mansion.

When we reached the third floor we had to line up single file to ascend the staircase to the cupola because of the narrowness of the stairway.

As we started to walk up the precarious staircase with me in the lead, a white, luminous mist began to form at the top of the stairs. The mist soon transformed into the rough outline of a person and started to descend down the staircase. As it did so, the crowd fell silent and I could see the look of wonder and terror cross their faces as they flattened themselves against the wall to allow the mist to pass.

As it made its way down the stairs, coldness emanated from the mist. Once at the bottom of the stairs, it disappeared. During this event I didn't stop talking about the history of the house, hoping the rest of the group would not pay the ghost of Jacob much mind.

Someone quietly asked me what that was. I didn't have a choice but to tell them it was Jacob, and he was just making room for us to view the cupola.

Half the group raced down three flights of stairs and out of the house, refusing to come back inside. The remainder of the group stayed with me, and they whispered quietly amongst themselves over what they'd just seen.

We ended the tour in the basement. I led them down the stairs and stood off to one side so they all could make it down the stairs safely. While I waited just outside the room with the dirt floor where I'd felt the horrible energy, the group continued to explore the basement.

Almost half of the people who came out of the room with the dirt floor told me they felt as if there was a body buried in that room. When I asked them what made them feel that way, they simply shrugged their shoulders and said they just had a feeling.

Their comments just begged the question: Was the spirit in that room of the basement simply so angry at being murdered, and the killer getting away with it, that it became hostile and frustrated?

An avenging spirit would certainly be capable of such energy; the feelings of hate, betrayal, despair, anger, and revenge would be almost unbearable. Or, alternatively, was the entity something more? Either way, I was more determined than ever to find out.

This was the first time that the possibility of a demon being in the house crossed my mind. Although at the time, I dismissed that thought. But I knew whatever the entity in the basement was, it was angry, full of hate, and really pissed off.

To this day, there has never been an investigation as to whether there was someone buried in that room or under the porch, so I can't prove that a body was buried there, but I can't prove there wasn't either. If, and that's a big if, there was someone buried in the basement, would that be enough to summon a demon?

My guess is yes, it probably would be. Suppose someone was murdered and buried in the basement. The act of murder itself is very negative and violent; just the type of energy that would attract a demon. Yet I can't let go of my feeling that the demon occupied the home for a number of years, and considering it never ventured into the addition of the home, with the exception of the apartment that Lisa used to live in, that tells me that the demon probably was there when the Matthews family occupied the house.

That fact alone raises some interesting questions as well. If someone was buried in that basement and the energy from that negative event brought in the demon, then one could possibly speculate that a member of the Matthews family was guilty of this. However, there is no evidence to this fact, and it's entirely possible someone was buried on the property long before the Matthews built the house.

Could this and the circumstances surrounding Mary Elizabeth's death be enough to keep Jacob from crossing over? Are these the secrets he still feels he must protect?

On the other hand, if there is no body in the basement or buried under the porch, then what could have brought the demon into the house? Unfortunately, these questions will never be answered, but it's still interesting to speculate.

Assume for a moment that someone held séances or used a Ouija board or some other divining tool in the house. It would be possible for a demon to enter the house if the people participating in these activities were inexperienced and they unwittingly invited or summoned the demon.

It's also possible that because of different kids and other people breaking into the house over the years and, according to stories circulating in the town, lighting candles and sitting in a circle attempting to raise the spirits in the house, that a demon was summoned there. The possibilities are almost endless.

CHAPTER TEN

As winter turned to spring, Susan and I began spending more and more time at the house on the hill investigating the Matthews family. It seemed every time we found the answer to one question, it only raised more questions about the family. We were becoming extremely frustrated, but we pushed on.

I kept returning to the house in hopes that Jacob would trust me more and start to share some of the family secrets with me, but to no avail. While he always seemed happy to see me, he was content just to have some company.

After a couple of weeks my life got busy with family and boating and Susan's and my investigation into the house fell by the wayside. This much-needed break only lasted a short time before something happened to suck me right back into the investigation.

One morning I was lying in bed waiting for my husband to get out of the shower and get ready for work. I was awake, but had my eyes closed. As I lay there I felt someone breathing in my ear in a slow and steady rhythm. The breath felt icy cold and it actually took a couple of seconds for what was happening to register in my head.

I could hear the water running in the shower so I knew whoever was breathing in my ear was not my husband. I quickly sat straight up in bed but saw nothing. I scanned the room with energy to see if I could detect any type of spirit, but all I felt was a little residual energy that vaguely resembled Jacob's energy from the Matthews house.

"What in the world was that about?" I asked myself, shaking off the bone-chilling cold that invaded my body.

Thinking maybe Jacob wanted to talk to me, I waited until my husband left for work and called Susan to ask her to meet me for breakfast and then go to the Matthews house. Over breakfast I told her what happened earlier that morning.

"Is it normal for ghosts to wake you up?" Susan asked.

"It's not unusual, that's for sure," I said. "Sometimes they just want someone to talk to, or want help, but no matter how distressed they seem, they are usually a lot more polite than the one this morning."

"How so?"

"They will gently poke me or tap me on the shoulder and then scurry to the end of the bed and patiently wait to be acknowledged. I've never had a ghost or any other entity breathe in my ear before."

We went to the Matthews house and raced up to the third floor to talk to Jacob. He denied being the one responsible, but I wasn't totally convinced. His energy seemed a little off, but I couldn't put my finger on how it felt different.

Now that I've had a few years to think about that morning, I'm pretty sure it was the demon that breathed in my ear and used Jacob's energy to throw me off the trail.

Susan and I eventually just shrugged off what happened as something we couldn't explain, and something we'd probably never get an answer to.

A week or so had passed since my last visit to the Matthews house when something similar happened again. I was again lying in bed waiting for my husband to get out of the shower. My eyes were closed, but I was fully awake. The sound of talk radio from the alarm clock droned on in the background and I really didn't pay too much attention to what was being said. Then I felt it again: someone was breathing in my ear with slow and steady breaths. My eyes flew open and I jumped out of bed only to realize two things: first, the clock radio wasn't even on, and second, there was no one but me in the bedroom.

I sat down on the edge of the bed perplexed. If the clock radio wasn't on, then who was in my bedroom talking? Wishing I'd paid closer attention to what was being said, I crawled back into bed to shake off the coldness that once again permeated my body. This time I kept my eyes wide open and my senses on full alert.

I waited until a halfway decent hour of the morning and called Susan to tell her what happened. After relating the incident to her, Susan and I were pretty convinced that Jacob just wanted company; that perhaps he'd gotten used to us being around and missed the human contact. We couldn't have been more wrong.

A few nights later, Susan and I were taking pictures in the cemetery, hoping that maybe Jacob or Mary Elizabeth would make contact with us so that we wouldn't have to go to the house. After having no success, we decided to take a ride by the Matthews house that sat about a half mile away because Susan wanted to take some more pictures. We pulled into the driveway of the house at about one a.m.

"Oh my God," I said as I got out of my truck.

"What?" Susan asked.

"You know that spirit in the basement?" I said.

"Yeah, what about it?" Susan asked as she put fresh batteries in her digital camera.

"Well, normally it doesn't leave the basement, but right now its energy feels like it's doubled in strength and is oozing out of the walls of the house. It's almost overwhelming. And the energy feels a lot like the energy of whatever breathed in my ear those two times, but not exactly the same—and it definitely doesn't feel like Jacob's energy."

"I don't feel anything. But let me know if anything changes." Susan began snapping pictures with her digital camera.

As I leaned against the bumper of my Jeep watching Susan, I began to feel nauseous, light-headed, and very weak. I felt as if the house was literally draining me of energy, like it was gearing up for something big.

"Susan, something's really wrong here," I said weakly. "I've got a really bad feeling about this."

"It will be okay. I'm almost done anyway. Don't be a wimp," Susan said half-jokingly.

I tried using my own energy to put up a strong enough shield in an attempt to block and push back the energy coming from the house, but no matter how hard I tried, I couldn't push this energy away from me and only succeeding in making myself feel worse.

"Susan, I feel really sick. We need to get out of here."

"Let's just wait a few more minutes and see what happens," Susan said.

I couldn't impress on her how serious I felt the situation was. The air almost crackled with electricity and every hair on my body stood on end. I felt raw anger and pure evil all rolled into one.

To get an idea of what this anger felt like, imagine yourself at your maddest and then multiply that feeling by about one hundred thousand and you're coming close to what I felt. I'm not sure there are adequate words in any language to describe what pure evil feels like. Suffice it to say that it feels heavy, oppressive, and filled with hate and loathing.

I looked up at the massive house and, between the two second-story windows, I saw an image begin to form. As I watched in disbelief an upside-down pentagram formed and shimmered like it was on fire. It looked as if the house was being branded by this symbol. I yelled weakly to Susan and told her what I saw, but she couldn't see it.

Having been taught Wicca by my mentor, I recognized the pentagram symbol and knew that when it was upside down, it could have different meanings. While an upside-down pentagram can represent the Earth, it is most often associated with Satan. Judging by the energy I was feeling, something really bad was about to happen.

As I stood there spellbound, staring at the pentagram, I saw it break open. A huge beast came out of the center of it, illuminated by the fire of the pentagram. The head resembled that of a wolf or some kind of large dog with red eyes, but much larger; it had long arms with two hands that looked like a combination of a claw and a human hand. What I could see of the body of the creature looked to be very large and muscular but not quite human.

Our eyes locked for what seemed like an eternity, but I'm pretty sure was really only a few seconds. To even try to describe what I saw in the eyes of that beast would be an exercise in futility, but here's the best I can do. I saw all-consuming evil in, what I believe to be, its truest form mixed in with a double dose of true fury. The intensity of the demon's eyes were unequal to even the dreaded "evil eye" that moms give their kids.

Something passed between the demon and me when our eyes locked on each other; to this day, I'm not exactly sure what it was. I want to say mutual respect, but that would be incorrect, for this demon didn't respect me in the least. I, on the other hand, immediately developed a healthy respect for it. I recognized true power when I saw it—a power that had to be respected.

I felt immense power that is unequal to anything else I've ever felt; it seemed to pulsate through the creature like blood races through our veins after strenuous exercise.

Then I felt something else, a wave of energy coming at Susan and I that was like a giant tidal wave heading for shore. The force and power behind this wall of energy immediately snapped me out of looking into the eyes of the creature. Right then I knew it was game on, and the stakes were high. I was truly convinced that if Susan and I didn't get out of there immediately, we'd never get out.

Just then the gray wolf appeared out of nowhere in front of me and started barking savagely at the force coming towards Susan and me. From somewhere I heard a voice yell, "Run!"

"Susan! Run!" I screamed. She must have heard the terror in my voice because for once, she didn't question me. She just ran towards my truck. I scrambled into the driver's seat and, with trembling fingers, got the key in the ignition and started the Jeep, backing out of the driveway and racing down the road. I didn't stop until we were at Susan's house.

On the way to Susan's, I told her what I'd seen and that I knew, without a doubt, the entity in the basement was a demon. I also tried very hard to bury how I was really feeling so as not to scare Susan anymore than she already was. But the truth was, I was shaken to the deepest part of my soul and was still trying to wrap my head around the fact that what I'd seen was a demon.

"You're positive you saw a demon," Susan said.

"Absolutely. What else could it be?" I said.

"This is really bad," Susan said.

"That's the understatement of the century."

"So what do we do?" Susan asked.

"I don't know yet. I need to think about this," I told her.

"We should probably stay away from the Matthews house until we have time to figure this out." Susan extracted three keys from the pocket of her jeans and handed me one. "Just in case," she said. It was a key to the Matthews house.

I dropped Susan off and raced home, taking a route that would let me avoid going past the house on the hill. I'd had my fill of that place for one night.

When I got home I raced to my computer and saw that a friend of mine who might be able to help was online. I instant-messaged him and told him what happened. Concern immediately filled his responses and he confessed he'd studied demonology for years. He asked me to describe the demon I'd seen and I described to him in as much detail as possible what the demon looked like.

He told me to go pour a good stiff drink and he'd get back to me in a few minutes. I wandered into the kitchen and poured myself a cup of coffee with a double shot of Irish cream and settled back down at my computer.

Within a half hour he returned and told me the demon I saw was Amon, which, according to Demonicpedia is a Marquis of Hell and the seventh of seventy-two Goetic demons who rules over forty infernal legions. For those of you who don't know, a legion is made up of approximately ten thousand demons. Further, Amon's appearance is that of a wolf with a serpent's tail, vomiting out of his mouth flames of fire. Amon is also said to be able to recall the past and reach into the future to see what is to come.

My friend also surmised that the wave of energy I felt coming towards me was, in all likelihood, some of the legions that Amon controls. He warned me to leave that house alone and to never return to it under any circumstances.

There wasn't a force on this earth that could have kept me away from that place after hearing all this. My curiosity kicked into high gear and I knew I had to learn everything I could about Amon. This was a decision I would come to regret in many ways.

As I sat sipping my heavily spiked coffee, I replayed the events of the night over and over in my head. What about the gray wolf? He jumped in and seemed to be trying to protect me; however, the fact that Amon can appear as a wolf still has me confused to this day. Was the wolf an animal guide protecting me or was the gray wolf really Amon, using his wolf form to make me trust the gray wolf?

As I write this, I now realize that Amon didn't come looking for me; I went looking for him. I'd had plenty of warnings from Amon to stay away from the house: the growling, the nightmares, being pulled back to the house in the restaurant that night. However, one could say that Amon lured me back to the house by these events, which would be a valid argument; still, I made a conscious decision to go back to the house. I could have walked away.

Yet now that time and distance have passed since that night, I can't help but wonder if Amon felt me slipping out of his grasp because my visits to the house were becoming more infrequent and he had to take desperate measures to pull me back into his intricate spider web.

I don't blame Amon that I made the choices I did in investigating the Matthews house, although I probably could. I only have myself to blame for not paying attention and refusing to believe that demons exist and weren't just a fabrication of organized religion.

Something happens to a person when their entire belief system is rocked to its core. Something deep inside your very soul snaps, and you are filled with feelings of panic mixed with blazing moments of clarity, but your brain is processing information so fast, you can't settle on just one thought.

Amon definitely rocked my world that night, and to this day I can't say I've fully recovered from it, although I can state with confidence that I'm a stronger person because of it.

However, if you run across what you believe to be a demon, don't be as utterly stupid as I was. Leave it alone and immediately seek professional help, whether from a member of clergy or a paranormal investigator. Don't, under any circumstances, try to face off with a demon yourself. You won't win.

There's a theory among most paranormal investigators and others that a demon or anything evil can't cross a line of sea salt. The theory behind this is that sea salt absorbs negative energy. This belief dates back to biblical times as a way of keeping negative energy from spreading.

If you want to take some precautions in an attempt to protect yourself from a demon, you can take some sea salt and sprinkle it *inside* your house by doors and windows. Start at one end of your home and work your way to the other end. Then you can sprinkle sea salt around the perimeter of your house. If you only put sea salt on the outside of your house, or put salt on the outside of your home before the inside, you will be trapping the demon inside your house. Not the result you'd be looking for.

Having strong beliefs and feelings for God could also help protect you from a demon. Note: being strong in your faith is not enough; you also have to make smart choices and not go out of your way to put yourself in the path of harm like I did.

Writing this chapter felt like reopening an old wound and in some way inviting the demon back into my life. I guess maybe I felt a sense of anticipation that the demon would return after all these years. I know what this thing did the last time it came into my life, and I'm not too enthusiastic about a repeat performance.

In fact, my office became very cold while writing this chapter; normally that's a sign there's some type of ghost or spirit present. While the weather outside was nice, and the rest of the house warm, my office was the only cold spot. I even changed from a T-shirt into a heavy sweatshirt, and I was still freezing. It was the kind of coldness that permeates down into the skin all the way to your bones. The air in my office felt thick, heavy, and oppressive and I felt it wrapping around me like a wet blanket. So I took a break and ran a very hot tub of water to try and get warm, but I sat in the bathtub shivering—the hot water not even able to cut through the coldness I felt. My skin felt hot when I got out of the tub, but the coldness in my bones remained. I quickly got redressed and made myself some lunch. I felt better after eating, but the minute I sat back down at the computer, my fingers became ice cold. I sat in front of the computer, freezing even though I was sipping a hot cup of coffee.

While I didn't sense a presence while writing this, that really doesn't mean much. I've always had a hard time picking up on Amon's energy when he's been around my house. It's like he can cloak it so I can't feel it real well. It gives him the element of surprise, I guess.

This was a very hard chapter to write. Having to relive that night took a lot out of me and has left me sapped of strength and mentally exhausted. But this book has to be written, and if I am being brutally honest, I'd have to admit I'm curious to see if the demon will show back up and if things will be different than they were the first time. I'm not so naïve, not afraid, and a lot stronger than I was when the events in this book took place, yet I can't help but wonder if that will make a difference.

CHAPTER ELEVEN

As the days passed, I spent more time at the Matthews house. This time it wasn't to talk to Jacob, or any of the other ghosts that inhabited the house, but to try to learn more about the demon.

My research showed that not only could Amon foretell the future, he could also recall the past and often reconciled arguments between friends. That didn't sound very demonic to me, yet Amon is also one of the highest-ranking princes of hell. My guess is that you don't get to that position by being nice if you're a demon. I surmised that if he did reconcile friends, it came at a high price. It is said that he's also the seventh son of Satan.

I also learned that some people believe Amon is the same as Amun, a God once worshipped by the ancient Egyptians. The Egyptians believed that Amun meant "hidden" or "that which cannot be seen," and he was associated with creation and the rising and setting of the sun and was a champion of the poor.

In my opinion, the Egyptian god Amun is not the same entity that I came in contact with at all. I tend to believe that the demon Amon, who seemed to delight in tormenting me, was indeed the seventh son of Satan.

What frustrated me the most was that while there are basic definitions and information about Amon, I could find nothing that told of his past deeds or actions. So basically, I was going into this blind. I set out to learn as much as I could about Amon by spending more time observing his behavior and actions.

It didn't take long to figure out that the demon rarely went farther than the first floor and the basement of the house; I never felt his energy on the second or third floors. However, his energy felt very strong and played heavily on my nerves and energy, leaving me feeling tired and drained. Perhaps he was protecting his nest or waiting for me to come to him.

Susan, still obsessed with the Matthews family, basically ignored the demon, partly because she couldn't feel him. She encouraged me to get back to work on the Matthews family. I tried hard to concentrate, but the constant energy of the demon kept distracting me, so I finally cut a deal with the demon: when I'm in the house, you stay in the basement and I'll stay out of the basement.

This arrangement seemed to work when I was in the house, but I should have been much more specific as far as other things. As strange as the whole situation seemed, things got even weirder as the days and months passed.

Many times when Susan and I were on the phone talking about the Matthews family and the house, the phone line would go dead. Sometimes, the same thing happened when I was on the phone with my friend Jesse, who lives out of state.

Susan and I wrongly assumed it was Jacob disconnecting the telephone. I now believe that this was Amon's way of trying to isolate me from my friends and family.

As I got more involved in figuring out the demon, more and more of my friends wanted me to take them by the Matthews house. It started with a woman I worked with. She came out one day and we drove to the house and walked around the outside. Two days later, her mother became deathly ill and almost passed away. People in Susan's family started to become ill as well.

While talking to my friend Jesse on the telephone, she related to me some dreams she'd been having about a specific house. When she described the house in her dreams I was struck by the fact that it was eerily similar to the Matthews house. Now why on earth would Jesse be dreaming about the Matthews house, a house she'd never even seen?

When Jesse came to visit later that summer, I took her by the Matthews house so she could see it for herself. She confirmed my suspicions. It was the same house as in her dreams. Soon after returning home, Jesse called and said her father became terribly sick and was in the hospital. He survived, but his health has never been the same and he's been in and out of the hospital frequently since then.

For me, that was the last straw. I was sick of this demon going after my friends. Late one night, I slipped out of the house and drove over to the Matthews house. As soon as I pulled into the driveway I could feel Amon's energy radiating around the outside of the house. Normally, this would be enough to give me pause, but not that night; I was pissed.

I jumped out of my truck and stormed up to the house. "Amon!" I yelled. "I know you're here, I can feel your energy! Stay away from my friends and their families; if you want to come after someone, come after me! I'm right here! But my friends and my family are off-limits! Do you understand?"

Without waiting for any type of response, I got back into my Jeep and peeled out of the driveway. On the way home I glanced in my rearview mirror and saw the gray wolf sitting in the backseat, staring back at me.

This startled me so much that I pulled off the road into the cemetery and stopped the truck. I sat for a few moments pondering the presence of the wolf. I didn't feel any negative energy coming from him, yet his sudden appearance right after I'd challenged Amon made me a little uneasy. I still hadn't determined if he was a spirit guide, a protector of some sort, or the demon himself, yet it had tried to protect me when Amon sent a few of his legions after me.

I turned and peeked in between the front seats of my truck back at the wolf, who now had inched closer to me. Our eyes met and I saw a mixture of quiet strength, power, and wisdom in his mesmerizing gold eyes.

"Thank you for trying to protect me from Amon's legions," I said.

The gray wolf bowed his head, breaking eye contact, and then disappeared.

It wasn't until the next day when I told my friend, David, the demonologist, about the events of the previous night that I realized it may not have been the smartest thing I ever did. David admonished me severely, not because I was trying to protect my family and friends, but because I challenged the demon. Apparently challenging a demon is something you should never do because, in most cases, the demon will accept the challenge and turn your life into a living nightmare. That was perhaps the single most stupid thing I could do, but in my defense, I didn't know it was wrong at the time.

This is not the proper way to handle that type of situation because anger is a negative emotion. It is also one of the strongest emotions and puts out a lot of energy. As I've said before, demons and some other types of entities feed off of any type of negative energy and/or situation such as emotional upset, drug abuse, alcoholism, jealousy, hate, etc. If fed this type of energy, they can become stronger and more powerful than ever imagined.

Fear is arguably the most powerful emotion, and will feed a demon or other type of negative energy, and, as hard as it may be, you should never, ever show fear to any type of ghost or spirit.

Your best course of action if ever in the presence of a demon or any other type of ghost, spirit, or entity is to be calm and assertive. There's a big difference between assertiveness and anger, so check yourself to make sure you're not projecting anger.

You can then say something like, "You're not welcome here and you don't belong here. You need to leave now. This is my house and I claim it in the name of _____ (whatever divine source you believe in, be it God, Jesus, Allah, Buddha, etc.)." Remember, don't yell at the entity, but speak in a calm and authoritative manner.

Another reason my handling of the situation was incorrect was that it also meant Amon had found my weakness and could, if he chose, capitalize on that and attack my friends and family even more. Something demons are known to do.

Little did I know that the words I spoke that day would start a horrifying chain of events. I wouldn't wish what happened to me on my worst enemy.

However, I often speculate about what would have happened if I hadn't told the demon to come after me. Would I be in the same position I am today? Worse off? Better off? I'll never know, but my guess is a lot more people would have been hurt until I figured out a way to stop it.

You know, I never told David about the gray wolf. I was worried he would make me send it away, and the mysterious gray wolf represented safety and protection to me. At that point, I firmly believed that all I had to hold on to were God and the gray wolf. But that's what demons do. They isolate their prey.

In fact, to this day, I've never even told my husband about the demon or the attacks on my friends. I told him about the house, obviously, and the ghosts that occupied the house but never about the demon.

There have been many times I've wanted to tell him, not only when everything was happening, but throughout the years since my encounter with Amon. I've even felt guilty about not telling him, but it feels like a heavy burden is resting squarely on my shoulders because I believe I have an obligation to keep not only myself safe, but him as well.

The demon already has had an effect on everyone else I've told, so logic would dictate that by not telling people about the demon, it would keep them out of his grasp. I believe my thinking is correct, because even now my husband and children have not had their lives touched by the demon in any way.

However, I am still so scared that the demon will go after my husband and/or my children. I can only protect them so much. Neither my husband nor my kids would be able to recognize the demon for what it is, and it could potentially destroy everything they've worked for all their lives.

Every second of every day I remain vigilant. I watch carefully and examine everything that goes on in my husband's life, as well as the lives of my children, looking for any sign of the insidious demon. Quite frankly, it's exhausting, but I don't dare let my guard down for that could be what Amon or some other demon is waiting for—just a sliver of an opening.

As I said before, my husband is not a huge believer in the paranormal, let alone demons, and quite frankly, I think he would be very angry with me for making the bad choices that allowed Amon to infiltrate my life, and, in a way, his life too. I couldn't blame him for being angry—I'm rather mad at myself as well.

Before every ghost hunt, he tells me that whatever I do, don't bring any of my "friends" home. How could I possibly tell him about the demon, knowing how he feels?

Earlier I wrote that demons like to isolate their prey. Obviously, this is what Amon did to me. By not talking to my friends and family about what was going on in order to protect them, I'd become isolated.

There are some people who will say I isolated myself by choice, and they'd be right. However, I'd been manipulated by the demon to make this choice, as there seemed to be no other option that would keep those I care about out of harm's way.

To this day, I'm still extremely reclusive, although I'm making a great effort to be more social and not live such a solitary existence. But I find myself keeping people at arm's length and not letting anyone get too close.

One of my closest friends suggested that maybe I need therapy to help me cope with what happened between Amon and myself. I'm not opposed to therapy, but am fearful that if I open myself up to a therapist, I wouldn't be taken seriously. I think a demon is one of those things that, unless it's experienced firsthand, one would be skeptical. The coping skills I'd learned as a child, having to hide my gifts from my parents, have proved to be invaluable when it comes to acting "normal" around my husband, friends, and family.

Now that I've written a few of the chapters about the demon, I can feel that he's crept silently back into my life in minor ways.

Nightmares are almost a constant companion now, and while I can't remember a lot of the details, I will wake up and sit straight up in bed drenched in a cold sweat. I try to stretch my mind to remember all of what happened in the nightmares, but to no avail. It's just the feeling that I've had a horrible dream, and it takes me a long time to get back to sleep.

Right now, sleep is important. I can't be in any type of weakened state knowing that Amon's energy is around me—that's what he wants—to get me weakened so he can strike again. Not that he won't anyway; it's just a matter of time.

I've resisted the urge to drive by the Matthews place; it's become too dangerous to do that now. That's where Amon's nest is, and if I've learned anything at all from running headfirst into a demon, I learned that you never meet them on their own turf. That's where they are the strongest; it's their power base. Yet if I had to be perfectly honest with you, I have driven by the house, many times. It's irresistible to me.

The dull headaches I've grown used to over the course of the last few years have become more frequent now, but not so bad that they are interfering with my daily routine. At least not yet.

A few of my friends have asked me how this book is coming; I tell them fine and then change the subject. I learned my lessons well and won't repeat the same mistake twice. Amon won't hesitate to go after anyone who gets close to me or in whom I can confide about what is going on or the contents of this book. That's why I was and still am so hesitant to write this story. I just don't know what the fallout will be.

Yet, I'm going to complete this book for several reasons, the first being that I won't let Amon have any power over me anymore. I won't let him control my actions and my life.

The second reason is that the story is too important not to be told, if only to warn others of what can happen if they run into a demon. Plus, it's time, I mean really time, to tell this story and go through the healing process of what happened to me. So in reality, this book is like therapy. Not a bad thing at all.

CHAPTER TWELVE

A week or so had passed since I had challenged the demon, and there were no repercussions. However, I had stopped talking about the house with my friends, and quit taking people by the house. In my mind, it was the only way to keep them safe.

Susan, in the meantime, was having her own set of problems. She'd discovered that her husband was having an affair and was, understandably, an emotional wreck. While we still talked, I refrained from telling her about the actions of the demon, believing she didn't need the added drama or stress in her life. At the same time, I couldn't help but wonder if the demon played a part in Susan's life falling apart.

I refrained from telling Susan anything about the demon since the night I first saw Amon because I felt it was the only way to protect her. So, despite my feelings of sympathy for her marriage situation, in a way, I was relieved to have her otherwise occupied so I could concentrate on learning more about Amon without the added worry about Susan's safety.

At this point, while he'd tried to scare me with limited success, my curiosity about the demon far outweighed any fear I may have felt. Plus, I knew from my years as a ghost hunter that some negative spirits grew stronger and more powerful if they sensed fear. So I did my best to keep what fear I had buried deep inside.

I decided the best way to learn more about the demon was to start out slowly—poke and prod gently until it elicited a response of some sort. The quickest way to accomplish this task was to break my deal with the demon about staying out of the basement of the house.

Armed with only a flashlight and all the courage I could muster, I made my way down the narrow, well-worn staircase to the basement. Years of wear left footfall impressions in the wood, which made the descent treacherous at best.

I got to the bottom of the stairs and turned left to enter the cinder-block room where Amon nested. Immediately, I felt the first wave of negative, evil energy hit me, and I steeled myself against it and moved forward further into the small room. In my mind, I called upon God and the Goddess to send down white light to protect me, and I envisioned myself surrounded by it.

I let my energy follow the path Amon's energy was coming from to try to discern where exactly the nest lay. Perhaps, I thought, if I can find out where the nest is, there would be a way to destroy it. It didn't take too long to figure out that Amon's energy was coming from the large, gaping hole in the far wall that led under the front porch.

As I continued to walk forward, the energy from Amon got stronger and became almost unbearable. I felt nauseous and slightly dizzy. When I reached a point about ten feet away from the opening, I heard a deep growl that seemed to come from nowhere and everywhere at the same time. It was the same growl I'd heard the first time I walked up to the front door of the house. Every hair on my body instantly stood on end, and a rush of adrenaline raced through my veins.

For a split second I thought about leaving, but knowing the demon would perceive that as a sign of weakness, I stood my ground. "It's going to take more than a growl to make me leave, Amon," I said, sounding a lot bolder than I actually felt.

Within a matter of a few seconds I felt the room become cold. Although it was close to eighty degrees outside, the temperature in the room felt like it was in the mid to low forties, and I started to shiver. This was an indication that an entity of some type was sucking all the energy out of the room in order to manifest or cause some type of activity. I quickly scanned the room but saw nothing out of the ordinary.

Upon taking a few more tentative steps towards the hole in the front wall, I heard a booming voice yell, "Get out!" Then, what felt like two unseen hands rested on my shoulders and pushed me roughly towards the door.

That was enough for me. I raced out of the room, up the staircase and out the backdoor of the house like I'd been shot out of a cannon. It wasn't until I was in the relative safety of my car that I stopped long enough to catch my breath.

Even though I'm a seasoned paranormal investigator, there are times when I just have to cut and run for my own safety. It wasn't so much that the demon yelled at me to get out; it was the hands pushing me backwards that let me know it was time to leave, especially when there's a demon attached to those hands. You may not win every battle, but you at least live to fight another day.

On my way home I started to think about what had just happened. I found it rather curious that the demon didn't do more. I mean, a demon is capable of extreme violence, so why did he act so passively to get me out of there? Obviously, he was protecting his nest just like anyone would protect their home against an invader, and I did encroach upon his space. Does that mean that a demon is capable of mercy? Or does a demon only use as much aggressiveness as necessary to get the desired result?

From what I'd read and learned from talking to David, demons try to control people in many different ways, intimidation being one of them. So was the demon trying to intimidate me to keep me away from its nest?

I'd also learned in my research that demons pick a specific target. It was obvious I was the target, so maybe he didn't become more aggressive because he couldn't afford to have his target disappear. He had to earn my trust in order to control me, and if he'd become more aggressive, it could have ruined his plan.

I'm still not sure which theory is correct, but I'm inclined to believe Amon was trying to control through intimidation and fear because every time he thought I was slipping away, he did something to draw me back in.

Don't misunderstand the demon's intentions. He could have done much worse, but since he'd already isolated me at that point, he didn't want to destroy the advantage he already had. Basically he was just protecting his home.

In the pre-dawn hours of the next morning I was awakened by something. I sat up in bed and looked around the bedroom, trying to figure out exactly what woke me up. Within a couple of seconds I was pushed violently down on the bed and pinned by unseen hands.

I tried to scream to wake my husband sleeping next to me, but no sound came out of my mouth, yet I could hear myself screaming in my head. Panicked, I didn't even think to try to feel the presence; I just knew it was poised on top of me and I couldn't move. In the next instant, I knew instinctively that it was Amon.

Everywhere the demon's body touched mine, it felt like my skin was on fire and every nerve screamed out in protest. I started to struggle to free myself, but the more I protested, the tighter his grip became. Not knowing what else to do, I relaxed my body as much as possible and called on the white light of heaven to shine down upon me. I then began to recite the Lord's Prayer in my head over and over, until finally Amon released his hold on me. I felt his presence scurry out of the bedroom, leaving me breathless and trembling.

I leapt from my bed and raced through the house to make sure the demon was no longer there. Once I was sure the house was clear, I sat down at my computer and took a couple of deep breaths. In all my years of ghost hunting, I hadn't been attacked like that since I was fifteen.

I went down the stairs to the kitchen and poured myself a glass of wine, then returned to my office on the second floor and slowly smoked a cigarette and sipped the wine, allowing the soothing liquid to calm my frayed nerves.

After a few minutes I found my friend David online and told him what had just happened. He spent the better part of an hour asking many questions about the attack itself, and how I got the entity away from me. We both agreed that Amon had come after me not only in answer to my challenge, which David admonished me greatly for, but also because I'd gotten too close to Amon's nesting place. He told me that under no circumstances should I ever go near a demon's nest. Many paranormal investigators and demonologists believe the nest is where the demon is the most powerful.

David also told me I got off lucky because it could have been much worse than what I'd just experienced. While the entire incident left me shaken, it also fueled my desire to learn more about how demons think and behave. However, I did learn that if you keep poking a demon with a stick, eventually it's going to poke back—hard.

I still relive every moment and every detail of the attack, trying to analyze it, to see if I missed anything. I have to admit it really scared me, and I don't frighten easily. While the whole attack was terrifying, the one thing that really stands out for me is the fact that I couldn't detect the demon's presence until it was too late. Since that time, I've been working hard to hone my gifts to the point that I can pick up Amon and other types of negative entities much faster.

I am still wondering if Amon was the same demon who attacked me when I was fifteen. The attacks were basically the same as far as tactics and viciousness, yet it seems highly unlikely that the two events are related. I mean, why wait over thirty-five years to attack again? Or could it be that Amon is the same demon and just stayed with me all those years waiting for another opportunity? As remote as this theory sounds, it's still a definite possibility.

Yet, somehow, I can't shake the belief that Amon resided in the Matthews house for well over a hundred years and is, in part, responsible for a lot of the tragic events that have taken place there—not just with the Matthews family but with almost anyone who comes into contact with that house.

David said it was possible that Amon was the same demon who attacked me years earlier, but it was equally possible that they were two separate demons. He went on to say that, while demon attacks can take on different characteristics depending on the demon's goal, the attack when I was fifteen and the most recent attack both have the classic markings of a demon attack: the inability to move or scream, and the feeling of an extreme adrenaline rush everywhere the demon's body comes into contact with a living person.

David went on to say that other signs of a demonic attack can include a sudden onset of depression; putting thoughts into your head that tell you to harm yourself or someone else; scratching sounds coming from walls, floors, doors, etc.; becoming argumentative or combative; the feeling of being physically and/or psychologically attacked by something and no one else feels it; and a general feeling of being creeped out. He told me to watch for any of these symptoms. Too late.

I knew I was feeling oppressed and my husband and I were arguing more and more about stupid things that really didn't matter, along with bigger issues like my ghost hunting and obsession with the Matthews house.

I wasn't even close to hurting myself or others, and I carefully monitored every thought that entered my head to make sure it was my own and not planted there by the demon, Amon.

The feelings of being under psychological attack were almost constant and it felt as if a dark cloud was wrapped around me like a wet blanket. No matter how hard I tried I couldn't shake the feeling of being constantly watched by something I couldn't see or feel.

I felt drained and tired no matter how much sleep I got, and I found myself taking more and more naps during the day. Some of this I attributed to the fact that I was out with Susan until the wee hours of the morning most nights, but I was really only fooling myself. I was under constant attack and didn't even realize it until years later.

The gray wolf became my confidant and I found myself keeping up a constant line of conversation when he was visible to me. I told him everything—my deepest fears about the demon and about the utter and total despair I felt in allowing myself to get into this situation.

The gray wolf would lie in my office snoozing while I talked and, every once in a while, he would open his beautiful eyes and give me a comforting glance, or walk over to where I was sitting at my desk and lie down at my feet in an effort to bring me comfort.

I couldn't decide if I was isolating myself from my friends and family or if they were isolating themselves from me because of my uncharacteristic mood changes and my long, solitary hours of brooding.

Not that they didn't try to break through this wall I'd put up around myself to protect them—they did try. I just wasn't feeling very receptive and was convinced it was the only way to protect my friends, my husband, and my children from the evil that insinuated itself into my everyday existence.

My husband, Kyle, and I were like two ships passing in the night in a deep fog—knowing instinctively the other was there, yet not making contact on any level. Amon had already done enough damage, and I couldn't imagine what else he could do to me that he hadn't already done.

CHAPTER THIRTEEN

Because of the apparent harsh retaliation by Amon for going so close to his nest, I thought it best to stay away from the Matthews house for a little while. I kept myself occupied with further research into the Matthews family, and tried to figure out a way to defend myself from the demon in case he attacked again.

Before I came up with a plausible plan, Amon did attack. This time I woke up from a sound sleep at 3:06 a.m. and became instantly aware of Amon's energy in my bedroom.

I sat up in bed and looked around, only to be forcefully pushed down again and held tightly. I felt Amon's weight on my stomach, and I couldn't scream or free myself from his iron-clawed grip. Everywhere his body came into contact with mine, it felt like my skin was on fire. I couldn't move, and I could barely breathe.

It felt like I was being sexually assaulted. I felt his hands rake across my body sending waves of energy deep into my veins. With every racing beat of my heart, the intensity grew as Amon's energy infiltrated every fiber of my being. The more I struggled to get free, the tighter his grip became.

In a single moment of clarity, I remembered the teachings of my spiritual mentor, Simon, and called upon the divine white light of God and the Goddess to shine down upon me and protect me. Within a moment or two the attack stopped and Amon fled from my house as quickly as he'd come, leaving me emotionally and physically drained of energy.

I leapt from my bed as if it were on fire and raced up the stairs to my office, then frantically searched for David online. Given the lateness of the hour, he must have been asleep, as he was nowhere to be found.

After a few deep breaths I'd calmed down enough to go back to bed and I lay there analyzing the latest attack.

It dawned on me that one of a woman's greatest fears is to be sexually assaulted. While I've never been assaulted in such a manner, I can imagine that the obvious violence and feelings of violation brought about by such an attack would take a great emotional and psychological toll on a woman, not to mention the deep-seated fear it must instill in a person. It's my belief that Amon, or any other demon, may use this tactic against a woman to make her feel vulnerable, afraid, and weak. This would enable the demon to control that woman with fear.

What amazed me most was the fact that my husband slept soundly next to me while all of the attacks occurred. David mentioned that Amon could have some ability to keep my husband asleep and undisturbed. It's possible that

Amon did this in order to keep me isolated. If my husband had witnessed the attack, he'd be forced to acknowledge that ghosts, spirits, and demons are real—something I'm sure he wasn't ready for. There is also the fact that, because my husband doesn't agree with my ghost hunting, he would blame me for bringing the demon into our lives by messing with things no one fully understands. My paranormal investigating already had put quite a strain on our marriage over the years, and I knew if he found out about the demon, it would be the final straw—we'd probably end up separated or divorced.

I knew I was playing right into Amon's hands because a demon doesn't want their target to have any confidant except the demon itself. It would make perfect sense that he had the ability to keep someone asleep and do everything he could to isolate me from everyone I know.

Exhaustion finally took over and I drifted back into a restless sleep only to awake late the next morning to find several bruises on my wrists and legs, along with a few scratches on my stomach. Thankful it was still cold enough outside to wear a long-sleeved sweatshirt and jeans, I knew I could hide the remains of Amon's attack from my husband long enough to let the wounds heal.

I also woke up angry—furious, in fact. So much so that I had to remind myself repeatedly that anger was a very strong negative emotion and could not only draw Amon to me, but make him stronger, so I spent an hour or so meditating to calm myself down.

Enough was enough; I decided it was time to take action and to stay away from the Matthews house until I'd grown stronger, more focused, and had a clear-cut plan in place to deal with Amon once and for all.

CHAPTER FOURTEEN

After spending countless hours on the Internet, I came to the conclusion that I was in for a real battle against Amon. What I was experiencing was spiritual warfare at one of its highest levels. That wasn't too comforting. I'm normally a very non-confrontational person, and having to fight a war was way out of my comfort zone.

I'm also not a very big believer in organized religion. I know God exists, and I worship him in my own way, but I don't attend church. I have a real problem with organized religion because I don't feel man has a right to dictate rules and interpret the Bible to suit his own needs. Yet, at the same time, I admire people who are devoutly religious and find comfort in their belief system.

A Catholic church sits near my house, and they have an oratory where people can go and pray, light candles, and perhaps find a few minutes of peace. I visited the oratory one day on a whim to light a candle for my father. I found the atmosphere to be calm and peaceful, and, for the first time in a long time, I felt safe. After that, I would visit the oratory about once a week and just sit in one of the pews and think about how to handle the situation with Amon.

One day while walking towards the oratory, I noticed a large statue of Jesus. He was standing with his arms out-stretched as if to give someone a hug. I must have passed by that statue every time I went to the oratory, but this was the first time it really captured my interest.

I found myself inexplicably drawn to the statue and stood looking at it for a long time. I felt some type of energy radiating from the bronze statue, pulling me closer. That energy was so strong, I felt like I was in the presence of another person. In a matter of seconds I found myself standing as close to it as I could possibly get and resisting the overwhelming urge to take the statue's hand.

A couple of minutes later I found myself putting my hand into the hand of the statue. I actually expected the hand to be warm and was shocked to find it very cold. Just as I placed my hand on the statue, the church bells chimed, jarring me out of the moment. I glanced at my watch—it was 1:05. An odd time for church bells to chime.

Anyway, the whole experience with the statue got me thinking—maybe it was God or Jesus's way of saying "you're not alone, I will be there to help you." I can't tell you how much comfort that experience brought to me. It did wonders for my mood and confidence—something I was rather short on at that moment.

But that got me thinking, was that all that was needed to win a high-stakes spiritual warfare battle against a demon? Faith? Prayer? A strong belief in God? It seemed too easy, although having God on your side can definitely tip the odds in your favor. But I also knew I'd gotten myself into this mess, and I would have to take steps to get myself out of it. I just wasn't exactly sure what steps those were.

I thought about seeking out a priest at the Catholic Church, but decided against it because I didn't know if he would have believed me. I am not by nature a very trusting person and have battled prejudice and being the "freak" because of my gifts almost my entire life. The last thing I wanted to do was set myself up for being judged and perhaps ridiculed.

That wouldn't do much to bolster my confidence or self-belief—the two things I most needed if I was going to be successful in my battle with Amon.

The most common type of remedy listed on the Internet when caught up in spiritual warfare seemed to be prayer. Nothing wrong with prayer, but it seemed a little too passive for me, so I decided I'd have to come up with some other form of weapon on my own. Not a physical weapon; spiritual warfare isn't fought with a tangible weapon. No, what I needed was a mental and spiritual weapon—that would be the only way I would stand a chance against Amon.

I talked to David and he said that I had the power to destroy Amon, but I would have to come up with exactly how to do that on my own and I had to believe in myself. He said to draw on all my training and my gifts and a way to take care of Amon would become clear. So I turned to my spiritual mentor, Simon, who lives in Wales. I'd known him a long time, and he had not only been my spiritual advisor but my friend. I often teased him about speaking in "Simon speak," better known as riddles that one had to decipher in order to glean any meaning.

While we were chatting online one day I explained the entire situation, leaving nothing out. He paid attention and asked a question or two while I related my tale; I asked him how I could defeat Amon.

Finally, he typed, "My dear, the answer you seek to the question you ask lies within. I cannot help you. But you already know what it will take to defeat this entity; you just have to be brave, trust yourself, and believe in yourself and what I've taught you—enough to use the weapons you have been given by God and the Goddess." With that said, Simon signed out and went offline.

I felt truly alone, as if the people whom I counted on the most when it came to matters such as these deserted me in my greatest hour of need. I sat for a long time having a pity party for myself and cursing Amon for taking away the last of my lifelines in the form of David and Simon. Both of them were more than willing to help me in the past, but they'd become distant and vague when I talked to them about the demon, and oftentimes cut our conversations short or changed the subject. They didn't want their lives touched by a demonic entity, and I really couldn't blame them. However, the more I sat and thought about what David and Simon said, the more I realized they were teaching me some valuable lessons—to be self-reliant, since no one can save you but yourself, and above all, to stay true to who you really are.

So I took stock of the weapons available to me—the list wasn't a long one. I could manipulate energy in various ways, I could "read" energy and determine if it was good energy or negative energy, if I focused extremely hard I could "see" certain energy, and I could see and communicate with dead people. I also had a working knowledge of Wicca, Paganism, and Christianity. Not a very impressive resume against a demon, but it was all I had. Now I just needed to figure out a way to turn my gifts and knowledge into a weapon that might give me an advantage over Amon.

Over the next couple of weeks I spent every available moment working with energy. I learned to manipulate my energy into balls the size of a grapefruit that I could to throw into the universe, and spent countless hours going to every haunted location—except the Matthews house— I could think of in order to hone my ability to pick up on spirits faster than I'd ever done before.

I focused on projecting my energy outward and using it as a shield against any energies that came towards me, repelling them backwards and forcing them to retreat.

But more than a month of this intensive treatment took its toll. I was physically, psychologically, and spiritually exhausted. No matter how much I slept, my body craved more sleep. However, sleep had its own set of problems. Horrible nightmares filled my slumber and any sleep I did manage to get was restless at best. I'd normally wake up with a start, in a cold sweat, frantically looking around the room for any signs of Amon. Then it would take me hours to get settled down enough to go back to sleep.

The only place I felt peace was at the oratory by my house. As I stated before, I'm not Catholic and don't care for organized religion, but at that point, any place that brought me a moment's peace was worth the effort to visit.

I'd spend hours in that small building thinking about how I was going to go up against something as powerful as a demon and, at the very least, come out with my sanity and what was left of my life intact. Although I have to admit, I did question my sanity several times and I wasn't entirely sure I had a life to go back to—well, at least a life I wanted. I prayed to God that I'd still have my husband, my friends, and my family when all of this was finally over—if it ever ended.

My extensive Internet research turned up a lot of people who believe as I once did, that demons are nothing but a fabrication by different religious-belief systems to keep their flock in line, or demons are just a reflection of something inside of us. Not exactly what I was looking for, but I respect the beliefs of others and moved on.

Then I found the other extreme where people were actually trying to summon demons in an attempt to control them or ask for favors. I couldn't believe it. Why anyone would consciously try to summon a demon was beyond any logical thinking.

In reality, it became increasingly apparent that, other than religious discussions about demons or Satanists who wanted to call demons forth from wherever they dwell, it was almost next to impossible to find any information I could use to my advantage against Amon.

I discovered that a lot of people who purported to be knowledgeable in demonic entities swore by the use of olive oil and/or holy water. The one common theme among all of these is that you have to totally believe in yourself, in whatever actions you choose to take, and that it will work.

One thing became readily apparent: I was in for the battle of a lifetime, and I couldn't fake it or make a half-hearted attempt to battle the demon.

CHAPTER FIFTEEN

I'd made the decision that the confrontation with Amon couldn't be at the Matthews house; it had to be on my home turf. That could give me the advantage—the extra edge I needed. At least I hoped it would.

I carefully thought out every step of my plan and tried to anticipate every move Amon would make based on his last two attacks, and how I could counteract them.

Knowing my husband was going out of town on a business trip in a couple of weeks, I scheduled the final showdown for when he would be safely out of the state and out of harm's way. I only hoped that I could lure Amon to my house in order to carry out my plan. The way I saw it, I only had one shot and I was going to put everything I had into it.

The day before I planned for the showdown with Amon, and with my husband out of town, I went to the store to get everything I needed. I bought one each of white, silver, purple, and black candles and stopped by the Catholic church to fill a small container with holy water.

My religious beliefs are drawn from many different areas, and I tend to use beliefs from Christianity and Paganism, so it took me awhile to decide on the colors of candles I wanted to use.

I chose white because it represents purity and aids in repelling negativity, silver because it can be used to remove evil energies and neutralize a space, and purple for protection and to ward off evil.

The decision to use a black candle was a difficult one. There are two points of view on black candles. One is that it represents retaliation, revenge, and can help with communication with spirits. The other point of view is that it can absorb and destroy negative energy and is often used in banishment rituals.

I tend to follow the latter viewpoint and, although it was a risky choice, in my opinion, it was a calculated risk worth taking. With everything ready, I got a good night's sleep in preparation for the battle I hoped would take place the following night. I'd told no one about my plan, for fear someone would try to talk me out of it. This was a spiritual and physical war between Amon and me, and there was no turning back.

The next day I put the candles on my nightstand, along with a lighter. I added the small bottle of holy water. I'd have to work fast, and I didn't want to have to scramble to find anything. Once everything was exactly where I wanted it, I drove to the Catholic church and spent more than an hour in the oratory asking God to guide me and help me through what was to come—to give me the belief and trust in myself that would be necessary if my plan was going to work.

I also took the time to call on my Pagan and Wiccan teachings and write a few simple spells to help me. I believe that spells written by the person who intends to use them are normally stronger than using someone else's spells because when you create them yourself, your energy and intent is intertwined in the words.

To tell the truth, I was a little worried about using Wicca to combat Amon. Not that I didn't think it would work—I was confident in the power behind Wicca—it was more because it had been a number of years since I'd used Wicca and I wasn't entirely confident in my skills; I was sure I'd become a little rusty.

But it was no time for self-doubt. It was imperative that I believed one hundred percent in what I was doing and was confident in my ability to perform the necessary spells in order to survive my battle with Amon.

After stopping at a local restaurant for dinner, I went to the Matthews house and let myself in through the side door just before sunset. Flashlight in hand, I purposely walked through the house and went to the room in the basement where I knew Amon was nesting. I'd felt his energy when I got out of my car, radiating from the house like the heat of a fire.

"Amon," I said, walking past the furnace towards the hole in the far wall. "I'm giving you one chance to stop attacking me and leave me alone forever. If you don't, I will destroy you. Do you understand?"

Without waiting for a response I turned and walked out of the room, up the stairs and out of the house, locking the door behind me. There was nothing left to do but go home and wait.

Somewhere around midnight I fell into a light sleep only to be awakened about 3:15 by the sound of a large dog barking wildly by my front door. I didn't own a dog at the time, so it was most likely the gray wolf warning me that danger was approaching.

I sat up in bed and heard the sound of light footsteps coming down the hallway towards my bedroom. I felt the powerful energy of Amon before he even set foot in the room.

In my mind, I saw Amon pause as he crossed the threshold into my bedroom. His energy felt overwhelming, and I only saw the shadowy outline of his wolflike body and head. He was standing on his hind legs. It took immense concentration to force the fear I felt deep down inside me. Suddenly, I questioned not only my plan but my sanity. For a split second, I wished I'd taken the time to really think this through and perhaps come up with an alternative plan of attack.

As his menacing figure slowly made its way along the foot of my bed, I pushed my doubts aside. I absolutely had to believe completely in what I was about to do, or it wouldn't work. The stakes were the highest they'd ever been, and I felt as if I was fighting for my very life. The entire bedroom filled up with the scent of rotten eggs. As soon as Amon got to the end of my bed and turned the corner to walk on the side where I lay, his figure disappeared. But I knew he was still there; I could feel him. As Amon's energy got closer to me, I became frustrated that I couldn't physically see him. I could only feel him.

I focused all my energy into a shield around me while I reached for the lighter on the table next to me, all the while aware that Amon was getting closer.

My energy shield didn't hold, and Amon's energy forced me down on the bed. I was completely unable to move. But I wasn't going to give up. I refocused my energy and was able to push him off of me enough to quickly sit up and light the white candle. I spoke calmly but forcefully, "In the name of God and the Goddess I do pray, Give me the ability and strength come what may, This demon must not stay, With these words I command him to stay at bay. So Mote it Be."

The temperature in my bedroom dropped sharply as Amon sucked the energy out of the room. He was trying to gain strength. It was so cold that I could see my breath.

Amon retreated just a few steps backwards, so I lit the purple candle and said, "This candle I light with its color so bright, May the divine forces higher than I release this candle's might, Send me guidance from above to take away the evil in my house this night."

The cold air in the room was almost debilitating. I shivered so much that my hands were shaking; I was having a hard time holding them still enough to light the candles. My teeth were chattering as I spoke.

I then lit the silver candle and said, "May all that is dark be filled with light, remove this demon from my sight. So Mote it Be."

My ability to hold off Amon became weaker, it felt as if he was attempting to use the energy shield I'd created to feed and regain his strength. I hadn't anticipated that, but kept going. I dropped my energy shield to prevent him from using my own energy against me. As soon as I dropped the shield, I could feel Amon's energy—it felt weaker than when he first arrived.

Finally, I lit the black candle. "This is it, Amon. It ends now. Almighty God, drive out of my life all evil spirits. Archangel Michael, please come to my assistance. In the name of Jesus Christ I command all demons to leave me be forever. In the name of the Father, Son, and Holy Spirit I command you, Amon…"

That's as far as I got before I stopped myself. Amon's energy was still in the room, but it felt weaker than before. I knew if I finished the prayer it would banish Amon back to the depths of hell, or kill him. I couldn't do it. My belief system wouldn't let me. To take Amon's life, such as it was, would make me no better than him.

We were at a stalemate. "Amon, I can keep doing this all night and send you back to where you came from or worse. You can take this one chance I'm giving you and leave me alone forever. While you have showed me little mercy, I'm not like you. I'm of the white light that represents all that is good and sacred; you are of the darkness and all that is evil. The choice is now yours."

I sat on my bed with baited breath waiting to see what Amon would do. I'd hoped I'd done enough, that my magic was powerful enough, and that I believed in myself enough.

That one little moment of doubt was all Amon needed. Before I could react, Amon pounced on me and held me down on the bed. My hands were over my head and Amon had them pinned down with one clawlike hand. I could feel his other hand rake my stomach. The skin on my stomach started to burn as he scratched me.

I was convinced he would show no mercy this time, and thought I was going to die. I tried to summon what strength I had left to use my energy and force Amon off of me, but it didn't work; it only served to enrage him more. His body became visible to me, and his face was inches from mine. I felt his foul, hot breath on my face. His wolflike lips curled up in an angry snarl, revealing his sharp, canine teeth. Sheer terror consumed my body, and I blacked out.

When I regained consciousness, I found myself kneeling on all fours in the center of my bed, hissing like a large exotic cat. I freaked out. What in the world was this?

I leaped off my bed and scanned the room for any sign of Amon's energy, but couldn't feel it anywhere. To be honest, I was more concerned about what happened between the time I had blacked out and came to than I was about Amon at that point.

I took the holy water off my nightstand and started sprinkling holy water ahead of me as I walked out of the bedroom and down the hallway towards the front door, all the while scanning for Amon's energy. There was no trace of it. Amon was gone.

I flopped down on the couch in the living room, gasping for breath. Every nerve in my body was tingling and waves of powerful energy pulsed through my veins. It took me a few minutes to slow down my breathing and get myself calmed down.

My mind was racing faster than the speed of light, trying to figure out what the hell had just happened.

Then I remembered what Simon had told me long ago about unity animals. He'd said that when you're born you're given a powerful animal that you can literally change or morph into in times of great peril or life-and-death situations. While you still have conscious thought, abilities, and intelligence as a human, you also have the skills and abilities of the unity animal.

To be honest, I didn't believe Simon when he told me about unity animals, but I really didn't have any other explanation for what I'd just experienced. To this day, I still have a hard time wrapping my head around what happened and the whole unity animal concept. Yet I can't deny what I myself experienced with Amon that night.

After having a glass of wine and struggling to come to terms with the events of the evening, I spent the next hour using the holy water to make the sign of the cross with my finger on all of the windows and door frames, asking God each time to protect this house, myself, and my family. Then I lit a smudge stick made up of sage, sweet grass, and frankincense and walked through every room, allowing the smoke from the smudge stick to infiltrate every nook and cranny. The battle was over, and while I'd won the battle, I wasn't entirely sure I'd won the war.

After I was sure I'd thoroughly smudged the house, I poured myself another glass of wine and walked into my master bathroom. The skin on my stomach was burning fiercely. I pulled up the T-shirt I'd worn to bed and saw three nasty-looking scratches running in a diagonal line across my stomach. I applied some antibiotic cream to them and curled up on my bed. I felt physically and emotionally exhausted and drained, but at the same time I felt exhilarated that I'd had the courage and confidence to do what needed to be done, even though I wasn't exactly sure what took place when I blacked out.

I awoke the next morning feeling much better. I'd slept deeply for the first time in months. The scratches on my stomach were almost gone, and the energy in my house felt lighter and fresh.

I just want to take a moment to say that, unless you are extremely confident and have experience getting rid of negative entities such as demons, you shouldn't under any circumstances do what I did in this case. Instead, you should seek the assistance of clergy or a good demonologist to help you get rid of any negative energy you feel is around you or occupying your home.

What I planned and executed was based on years of experience ghost hunting, performing house clearings, and the spiritual teachings of Christianity, Paganism, and Wicca, all of which I've been taught by various people throughout the years. The rest was just gut instinct and something else I still can't quite explain.

CHAPTER SIXTEEN

A couple of weeks after my showdown with Amon, I got a telephone call from Susan. She told me that Lisa sold the house to a man who wanted to renovate it or tear it down and rebuild. I felt panicked and distraught. I wanted that house to live, to continue to stand where it had for more than a hundred years. In spite of Amon, the house had significant historical relevance.

I hung up with Susan and started making some calls of my own. I called the realtor who'd had the house listed, and she agreed to contact the new owner to see if he would speak to me.

I then contacted the state historical department and talked to a few people there who, while they felt for my situation, told me that the likelihood of the house being saved was slim, but suggested that a structural engineer be called in to render an opinion on the integrity of the home.

Less than an hour later the new owner of the house, Mr. Davis, telephoned and we had a nice discussion about whether the house could even be saved. I relayed the advice of the state historical department, and he agreed a structural engineer's report would be a good idea. He promised to let me know when the inspection would take place.

I found out there would be a hearing by the city to make a decision on whether or not they should order the demolition of the Matthews house. I attended and spoke at that meeting, and came up against strong opposition, mostly from a woman who lived by the Matthews house. Mr. Davis and his attorney were at the meeting and convinced the city to hold off on any decision until after the structural engineer had a chance to inspect the property. The city agreed.

Personally, I had my doubts about the structural integrity of the house given the fact that some of the basement walls seemed to be in bad condition, and large cracks ran up and down the brickwork of the house, causing a couple of the outside walls to have the appearance of buckling. Combined with the fact that all the floors in the house seemed to be slanting inwards towards the center of the house so much that one got the impression the house was ready to implode on itself, I didn't hold out much hope that the house could be saved.

The following week Mr. Davis called and said the inspection was scheduled for the next day, and that I was welcome to attend since I knew the history of the house better than he and could supply the engineer with more information. I readily agreed to meet them the next day, even though I was a little apprehensive about going back to the Matthews house after my showdown with Amon.

Early the next morning I pulled into the driveway of the Matthews house to meet Mr. Davis and the structural engineer. I answered some of the engineer's questions, such as the age of the original structure and when the addition was added. The engineer said his inspection could take up to four hours to complete. I declined to enter the house, saying I had errands to run and would be back at the conclusion of the inspection to hear the results.

I leaned against the hood of my Jeep to take a few minutes and feel the energy of the house. The house felt sad, as if it knew the inevitable was coming and there was nothing more it could do to save itself. I walked around the house and paused when I reached the far side of the front porch. I knew just underneath my feet lay the nest of Amon. I felt his energy radiating up through the ground. Even though his energy was weak, I knew it wouldn't be long before he regained his strength. I only hoped my plan had worked and he would leave me alone. I got into my truck and drove home to wait.

When I returned to the Matthews house four hours later, the engineer said that while the original footprint of the house might have been salvageable, the addition was in a weakened state and would have to be demolished. Then the original house would have to be lifted off its foundation, a new basement and foundation put in place, and the house lowered back down. He went on to say that the odds of the house surviving such construction were less than forty percent, and it would be extremely expensive.

I knew right then and there the house was going to be demolished, and I asked Mr. Davis if I could go through the house one more time. He agreed and asked me to lock the door on my way out.

He said that eventually he would build two houses on the one-acre parcel of land; one for himself and one for his son.

I wished him well and cautiously walked into the Matthews house for what I knew would be the last time. As soon as I crossed the threshold from the apartment into the original part of the house, a blast of very strong, angry energy surrounded me.

It wasn't Amon's energy, it was Jacob's, and he was furious that his once-glorious mansion was to become nothing but a pile of rubble. What struck me as odd was that Jacob had never previously left the third floor. I'd never felt his energy anywhere else in the house until that moment.

As I climbed the stairs to the second floor I spoke aloud and explained to Jacob the reasons behind the decision to tear down the house he loved so much, and that it was time for him to rejoin his family on the other side.

No matter what I said, it did nothing to quell the anger I felt emanating from every corner of the house. I told Jacob that I'd done everything I could to save the house, but the house just couldn't be preserved.

When I turned the corner of the staircase to ascend to the third floor, I felt Jacob waiting for me at the top of the stairs. The energy from his anger almost made me stop in my tracks, but I continued on.

When I got to the third step from the top, I had a vision of myself being levitated into the air and thrown over the railing only to land three stories down. I know without a doubt Jacob put that vision in my head as a warning; but a warning against what? Jacob had never threatened me before. Or was he trying to warn me about something else?

I turned around and went down the staircase to the second floor and then stopped. "No," I said, "no ghost is going to scare me out of this house again." With newfound determination, I retraced my steps and began to run up the stairs to the third floor. Jacob, in turn, began to come down the stairs towards me, his rage and energy growing stronger by the second.

It was then, and only then, that I felt something different in Jacob's energy, something familiar: I felt Amon's energy begin to manifest and push Jacob's energy out of the way. I knew right then I'd been caught off-guard, and I knew what Jacob had tried to warn me about.

I stood frozen on the staircase. I felt Amon's intense rage and hatred radiating towards me just a few stairs away, and I knew I had to make a choice. I could stand my ground and fight, or I could run out of the house in fear.

My mind was racing. If I stayed and fought, Amon would win. If I turned and ran, Amon would win. Then I thought of a way for me to get out of this and end with a stalemate.

I took a couple of deep breaths to calm myself down and concentrate on gathering every ounce of energy I had; I put that energy around me in an effort to protect myself. I held out my hand towards Amon in an attempt to use my energy to hold him at bay.

"Amon, I'm in control of this situation, not you," I said with more confidence than I felt. "I'm choosing to leave you in peace. The house will be demolished and your nest destroyed. It's time for you to go back to where you came from and leave me alone forever."

As I spoke I felt Amon's rage growing and the stairway became ice-cold. I felt my invisible energy shield weakening against the force Amon was putting on it, and I could feel Amon increase his energy as if he was getting ready to attack. It felt like all of his energy recoiled and then spun into a tight tornado and entered his body, making him the strongest I ever felt him. I instinctively knew if I stayed any longer something really bad was going to happen. I didn't want to stick around to find out what would happen because I knew it wouldn't end well for me.

Being on the stairs put me in a rather precarious position, and I knew I only had one option left. I turned and ran down all three flights of stairs and out of the house, pausing only long enough to lock the bottom lock on the apartment door.

Once safely back in my Jeep, I pulled out of the driveway and drove to the cemetery down the road. I pulled through the gates and stopped the truck. I had to catch my breath and stop to think. I got out of my truck and flung myself down on the ground between Mary Elizabeth's and Jacob's tombstones.

I don't know why I blindly drove to the cemetery and ended up at their graves. It wasn't as if they could protect me from Amon; they couldn't even protect themselves. Yet, at the same time, I felt comforted by the fact that their bodies lay just below me in the cold ground. Maybe it was because they were my last tie to the house, and that they would in some way understand what I was going through.

In fact, I was a little disappointed that neither of them made an appearance or even tried to communicate with me. If they had, it would have brought me such comfort, knowing that they understood and that I wasn't alone in this. But there was nothing. It was like they, too, didn't want to get too close to me for fear of Amon's thirst for vengeance, as if that evil might turn away from me and go after them. I guess I couldn't really blame them for feeling that way. I often wished I could escape the nightmare that had become my life.

As I sat there in the silent cemetery, I wondered if it could all have been an elaborate illusion. Was Jacob a disguise for Amon to gain my trust and keep me coming back to the house? That could explain why Jacob never answered my questions about how Mary Elizabeth died; he probably didn't know, and if he did, he wouldn't have told me for fear I would no longer visit the Matthews house and he would lose his grip on me. It all made sense now and made me wonder if he'd portrayed the ghost of Mary Elizabeth as well.

However, looking back on it all, it could be that the ghosts of Mary Elizabeth and Jacob were really in the house, but were being manipulated by Amon, just as I had been. This wasn't beyond the scope of Amon. I wondered if I'd ever really know for sure.

My gut tells me that Amon did not impersonate Mary Elizabeth or Jacob, yet there's still a cloud of doubt that clings to that issue to this day.

I sat by the graves and sobbed uncontrollably at the thought of that once-glorious mansion being destroyed, of knowing that I'd never be able to set foot in that house again or converse with Jacob or Mary Elizabeth. I worried about what would happen to Jacob once the house was gone. Would he finally go into the light and join his wife and daughter? Or would he simply move into a neighboring house and haunt the innocent people living there? When I really thought about it, those people were not so innocent. They wanted the Matthews house gone, so perhaps they should learn the lesson I learned so harshly: be careful what you wish for, because you just might get it.

And what of Amon? Would he continue to stay on the property or would he, too, move on to more fertile hunting grounds? That thought terrified me because he could have come back and invaded my life once more, or go forth into the universe and prey on more innocent people. That's my only regret in not destroying him when I had the chance. By my letting him survive, he lived to fight another day. His next victim may not be so lucky.

Yet, could I really have destroyed him? I doubt it. I think the most I could have done was to banish him back to wherever he came from, and even then, I don't think it would have been permanent. I think he would have risen again and sought out his next victims no matter what I did. With an entity that powerful, any human who thinks they can destroy such a demon so it never returns to earth is, unfortunately, fooling themselves, or deluding themselves because it makes them feel better.

Maybe the living are able to banish demons for a while, but how can you kill something that was never alive to begin with? You can't. The most any living person can hope for when faced with a demon is to do enough to keep the demon out of your life permanently.

As you can tell by this story, permanently doesn't always work.

After about an hour of lying between Jacob's and Elizabeth's graves feeling sorry for myself, I pushed aside the feelings of despair and sadness and decided to pick up whatever pieces of my life were left and move forward. Because that's all any of us can do when met with trauma. We can't go back; we can only move forward and carry on the best we can.

I got up off the ground and wiped my eyes on the sleeve of my sweatshirt. I paused just a few seconds more to pay my respects to Mary Elizabeth and Jacob and wished them well before walking slowly back to my truck for the short drive home.

A week later the Matthews house met the wrecking ball and it took less than an hour for the house to come down.

I was there the day the house crashed to the ground in a cloud of dust. Several townsfolk, including myself, collected some bricks from the house as it lay in a crumpled heap—keepsakes from a bygone era and a once-magnificent home.

I did notice one thing, though—the basement of the Matthews house was filled in with rubble from the house; the basement wasn't removed. Amon's nest was still intact! My first thought was one of panic. Amon would live on just a few miles from my home. Just when I thought it was over, perhaps it really wasn't.

My second thought was, "May God have mercy on the souls of anyone who builds on that land, and I hope they lose my telephone number." I'd had my fill of the Matthews house and the demon that dwelled deep within its bowels. I wanted my life back. I wanted to be able to sleep again and be happy—although happy is a relative term. What I really wanted was peace; a peace I'd lost somewhere on this long and arduous journey.

Two weeks later I was in the antique store in town and overheard a woman talking to the owner of the store. They were discussing the demolition of the Matthews house; I pretended to be enraptured by an antique French vase so I could overhear their conversation.

The woman said that she lived behind where the Matthews house once stood and ever since the house was torn down, they'd been hearing footsteps, like someone was walking with a cane going up and down the stairway to the second floor of their home, and they had been hearing strange noises coming from their crawlspace and attic. She went on to say that they'd called an animal-removal company, but no trace of any type of animal was found anywhere in the house, including the crawlspace and attic.

I couldn't help but chuckle to myself. My questions were answered. The ghost of Jacob really had occupied the Matthews house and when I felt Amon's energy coming from the spirit I thought was Jacob, it probably was the only time he'd taken Jacob's form. At least I hope it was. If not, the lady in the antique store was in for a lot of trouble.

I know I should have talked to her and told her about the demon, but I didn't. She'd been one of the main people fighting to get the house torn down. My heart tells me I probably should have told her what was going on in her house, but I just couldn't bring myself to do it. I still felt bitter towards the people who fought so hard to bring that house down when I fought so hard to protect one of the last pieces of history in that town.

While I logically understood their point of view, emotionally I felt attached to that house in a way I'd never felt attached to anything or anyone in my life before. I felt as if I'd finally come home and belonged somewhere and that had been brutally ripped from my grasp.

Don't misunderstand; I love the life I've built with my husband and children, but there's always been this deep-seated feeling of never belonging anywhere until the day I walked into the Matthews house. The Matthews house and, yes, even the demon Amon, will always be with me in some way. I don't think anyone can go through what I did and not have it become a part of their soul; part of what makes them who they are; and who they will become in the future. It would be foolish to think otherwise, even if one tries to deny that such an event could leave them untouched and the same person they were before it happened.

I don't waste time trying to delude myself in such a fashion. Life is too valuable and too short to give in to such frivolous thoughts. I now treasure every moment I have with my friends and family, for I learned the hard way that everything you have can be taken away in the blink of an eye, or in one act of curiosity.

THE AFTERMATH

I am pleased that the final confrontation with Amon was the last major one… so far. But I know he's still around. I feel his energy at times in different places, but I feel no serious threats to the safety of myself and my family, and there have been no more attacks since the night I let him walk away.

Both David and Simon were angry with me for not finishing Amon off, but there's nothing I can do about that. I know in my soul that I made the right decision.

Two years ago David got brain cancer. He died a short time later. Simon has just recently been diagnosed with a rare type of narcolepsy and is in poor health. I am still very healthy and going strong. I'm not saying that Amon is responsible for David's and Simon's illnesses. I'm simply relaying facts without any judgment.

There have been signs that Amon is still around. For example, my husband and I were at a gas station one day after doing our grocery shopping and it was raining extremely hard. The rain cascaded from the roof over the gas pumps down to the ground and, while my husband was pumping the gas, I waited patiently in the car, thinking about what I had to do when we returned home from the grocery store.

I heard the rain dropping onto the windshield and glanced up. There was a light fog that covered the windshield because of the rain. Letters were written into the light fog. A M O N. I gasped in shock. Amon must have been right there and I hadn't even felt him. I quickly turned the key just enough to get the windshield wipers to erase the writing so my husband wouldn't see it, but it shook me up. I'd allowed myself to be lulled into a sense of false security because he hadn't attacked in more than eight years. I should know better than to let my guard down—ever.

A few times I've been awakened late at night and felt Amon's energy in my bedroom. The minute he realizes I'm awake, he leaves. That doesn't happen too much since we've moved, but it does happen.

Amon still invades my dreams at times. I'll see him in the background, letting me know he's still around and I'll never truly be rid of him. I would like to think that he has a newfound respect for me because I spared his life at our last meeting, but that would be egotistical and foolish. I don't think Amon respects human life, but rather views humans as prey, like a wild animal hunts down and kills for food.

I do take precautions to protect myself from Amon. I smudge my house once a week and take regular cleansing baths with a homemade mixture of sea salt and rosemary and sage oils to wash any negative energy off my body.

If I do happen to feel Amon's energy around me, I light white, purple, and black candles and use a modified version of what I said the night I squared off against him: "These candles I light with their flames so bright, I ask that God and the Goddess release these candles' might, Send me guidance from above to dispel the evil in my house tonight."

I often wonder about the gray wolf, and whether his purpose was to protect me, or whether he was Amon in disguise and he appeared as the wolf to keep an eye on what I was doing.

It's also possible that Amon would disguise himself as the gray wolf and would jump in front of his own legion of demons, knowing full well that I would be long gone before he would ever have to stage a battle with the legions. It's something Amon would do to earn my trust.

My gut is telling me the gray wolf was some sort of spirit guide, or spirit protector, that showed up in my time of need—as spirit guides will do—yet I still have lingering questions about the wolf, such as why he didn't show up and protect me while Amon was attacking me in my own home, or why he hasn't been seen since. Perhaps the threat is over and the gray wolf didn't have a need to show up anymore. I'll never really know, I guess. Just like the Matthews family, the gray wolf has left me with more questions than answers.

So the last ten years haven't been too bad… at least during the day. It's the nights… those are the worst. My battle with Amon has left a psychological scar that will probably never quite go away.

There are nights I sleep just fine; then there are the nights when my body wants to sleep, but I resist sleep because I know that could be the night the evil creature sneaks back into my dreams and reminds me of what got me into that mess. Yet I sleep…almost. Even though my body is sleeping, my conscious mind is constantly monitoring my dreams… just in case.

When Amon does show up while I'm sleeping, I fight to wrestle myself into total consciousness and lay awake the remainder of the night wondering if it was just a dream, or perhaps something else. A warning? I'm never sure if it's really Amon himself, or just my subconscious mind trying to reconcile what happened with Amon, although there have been a few times I've awakened from one of these "dreams" and felt the residual energy of him in my bedroom.

Again, on those nights I lie to myself and tell myself it was just a dream, that I'm being irrational, and letting my imagination get the best of me, just so I can get the sleep my body is craving. Yet, at the same time, I fight sleep for fear the demon will return. Finally, I fall into a restless slumber out of pure exhaustion, yet my mind is still on guard against another onslaught from the creature that turned my life into a living hell.

I will wake up with sore muscles from my body being tensed up most of the night, bracing itself in case the demon attacks, and with a dull headache that I've learned to ignore. I spend a lot of time being ever vigilant against any little sign the wretched creature that invaded my life has returned once again, although that happens less frequently now.

Every once in a while I'll drive to where the Matthews house once stood and get out and walk the property, looking for any sign that Amon is still nesting there or whether he, too, has moved on to more fertile hunting grounds now that there is no longer any energy left for him to feed on. I do this mostly out of curiosity, but I think it's also to remind myself of what can happen when I let my curiosity override logic.

Occasionally while I'm at the property, I'll feel Amon's energy, but only briefly, and I'm not sure whether he's still there permanently or only there because I'm there. I often wonder if my presence there is enough to call Amon back to the property. I'll never truly know the answer to that question.

The bricks I took from the Matthews house are still sitting in the corner of my office at home. They are filled with the energy of that house. I'm not even sure why I kept them, why I was so desperate to possess them.

I tell myself that the bricks are here to remind me what happened, and how naïve I was during most of the time I spent dealing with that house. I don't want to forget what happened. I want to remember how stupid I was and to never be that way again.

But in reality, they are here to keep me tied to the place I just can't let go of—or maybe it's the other way around; maybe it's not ready to let me go. Maybe the house keeps itself alive through the collected bricks taken by the towns-people.

Some of my friends have told me to get rid of the bricks. That's something I just can't make myself do. Others have suggested that I cleanse the bricks to remove all the residual energy. If I did that, what would be the point of keeping them? I want to feel the energy of that house.

Logically I know I should get rid of the bricks because they could be what draws the demon back to me. The energy of the bricks, like all energy, sends out a signal, and it could be that the bricks are acting like a homing device that Amon can use to find me. But emotionally, I am as attached to those bricks as Jacob was attached to his home. I just can't bear to let go; the house and its phantom inhabitants are a part of my soul now.

Susan had moved away a year or so ago, but she came back into town recently and we met for coffee. She told me her daughter had gone by Mary Elizabeth's grave and noticed that someone had poured salt around the perimeter of the grave and on top of the grave. One of Susan's daughter's friends had also reported seeing salt around Mary Elizabeth's grave.

As I stated before, sea salt is supposed to keep negative spirits or other evil types of entities out of a place. There's a theory that a negative entity cannot cross a line of salt. However, if a negative entity is already in your home or place of business, salt will trap them there.

Putting salt around a grave is an act of someone who is scared to death and desperate. The question is, who put it there and why? Especially on Mary Elizabeth's grave—she wouldn't hurt a fly.

When I first heard of this incident I thought it was just kids; however, it happened twice. Generally kids will only pull a prank like this once and it loses its charm.

No, this is an act of someone who is truly scared and believes for some reason that Mary Elizabeth is responsible. My best guess is that this person lives around where the old house once stood and is having trouble with spirits and assumed it was Mary Elizabeth. Maybe they even saw an apparition of a young woman dressed in Victorian garb, which could be Mary Elizabeth and, whether or not this spirit acted out, it could have so badly scared the person who saw it, they assumed it was evil. The other possible explanation is that the demon is impersonating Mary Elizabeth.

I'll probably never know what motivated the person to pour salt around Mary Elizabeth's grave, or if they've repeated this behavior since then. My guess is that they have and will continue to do so until they find someone who can help them figure out what's going on in their home.

In the end, this is just one more mystery to add to the other mysteries surrounding Mary Elizabeth and the Matthews house. Susan and I never did learn why Mary Elizabeth was buried under the name of Gibbons, or what sordid past the town was desperately trying to hide. Now with the house gone, it seems like we may never learn.

Just recently, I was getting ready to clear a ghost out of a client's house and checked my bag to make sure I had everything I needed. It was then I discovered that my cross and rosaries were missing. I always keep at least one rosary and one cross in my ghost hunting bag.

I did a quick search of my jewelry box, bathroom drawers, and anyplace else I could think of in the limited time I had, but couldn't find them anywhere.

When I got back from the house clearing, I did a more complete search but still couldn't find any of them. I know demons are capable of moving, throwing, or destroying religious articles and/or making them disappear altogether, but it still stunned me to discover all of mine were gone.

I spent the next two days searching the house and still saw no sign of my rosaries or my cross. Three months later I was doing a routine dusting of my bedroom and was dusting a bedroom stand. It's a small stand with a mirror and two candles on the top, a large open wooden circle for a large bowl, and a round shelf underneath the bowl down at the bottom of the stand, not just for stability, but to place a large pitcher on.

When I moved the pitcher I heard something rattle inside of it. I found one of my rosaries in the bottom of the pitcher. I was totally confused. There wasn't any way one of my rosaries could have fallen into that pitcher nor would I ever put anything in that pitcher.

In addition, I'd dusted that shelf every week and moved the pitcher every time. I would have heard the rosary rattling around in there long before then.

As I was putting the finishing touches on this book, I found my other rosary. It fell out of my medicine cabinet when I opened it one morning. I open that medicine cabinet every morning and can attest to the fact that it wasn't there. My husband has his own medicine cabinet and never goes into mine.

I did, just for the sake of argument, ask my husband if he put the rosary in my medicine cabinet, and he said he hadn't. I still haven't found my cross.

Someone once asked me if I could go back in time to before I got involved with the Matthews house, would I? The answer would be a definite No!

While what I experienced was terrible, I learned so much during that time—not just about myself, but about demons. Now it's up to me to take that knowledge and help other people. That's the good that comes out of the situation.

What happened between Amon and me helped make me the person I am today: stronger, wiser, and able to face just about any situation. I mean, if I can face down a demon and survive to tell the tale, I can survive just about anything.

To you, the readers of my story, I wish you health, happiness, and life free of demons. I ask that you listen to your instincts, and if you feel that something isn't quite right, pay attention and get out of wherever you are. Don't go back.

I know there will be some who read this book and will not believe my story, and that's fine. I didn't believe in demons either until I met one.

However, it's been my experience that just because you don't believe in something doesn't mean it doesn't exist and can't reach out to you in the dark hours of the night, or the bright light of day, and attack you when you least expect it.

EPILOGUE

While working on this book, I kept track of anything out of the ordinary that happened. Some of these events I put into the book, but some of them just wouldn't fit so I've included them here.

FIRST EXPERIENCE

As I started working on the book, I drove by where the Matthews house used to be. I was on my way back from a ghost hunt and just couldn't resist the pull I'd been feeling from where the Matthews house once stood. I'd driven by the property many times since the house had been destroyed and very rarely felt anything.

I arrived at the land and got the same feeling I used to get. There was something there. I felt this huge blast of energy hit me hard as soon as I pulled into the driveway, like being hit upside the head with a two-by-four.

I couldn't help but wonder if some part of the house lived on; I mean, they didn't take out the basement. Is it possible that the soul of the house survived the demolition and was letting me know it was still alive; still vibrant, just lying dormant waiting for something? Could it be that just like with living creatures, the body dies but the soul lives on? My first thought was that it could have simply been residual energy from the house, but residual energy doesn't smack you upside the head like this energy did.

Once I recovered from that, I felt the demon, Amon. I'd know his energy anywhere. It felt thick, heavy, evil—not just bad, but pure evil. It's so intense that unless you've felt it, you wouldn't really understand it, and words fail to describe how pure evil, hate, and anger feels.

It actually caught me off-guard. I really wasn't expecting Amon to be there. I wondered if I drew him back by thinking about writing this book. I'm still not sure. Could that energy have been the house trying to warn me to stay away, that there was still danger there? I suppose it's possible.

Anyway, I sat in my car for a few minutes contemplating what I should do. I could get out of my car and walk the land—see if the beast reacted. But it was already one o'clock in the morning and I was tired. I decided against it and eased my car back onto the road to drive home. I know from experience that the worst time to face a demon or any other entity for that matter is when you're tired.

The next morning I drove back to the Matthews house in search of the source of the energy I'd felt the night before and the mighty demon, Amon.

I backed into the driveway just in case I had to make a quick exit and ignored the No Trespassing sign as I walked up the driveway towards where the house once stood.

This time, no wall of energy rushed out to greet me as it had the night before, but I could feel the energy from the house just under the surface of the dirt and grass. The energy was coming from the basement, but it wasn't Amon's—it was what was left of the house buried just below the surface of the earth.

As I walked, I let my gifts take over and sent waves of energy down into the ground, searching for any sign of Amon. It's kind of like a sonar wave on a submarine putting out tendrils into the sea searching for the enemy.

I could feel Amon's residual energy, which told me he'd recently been in his nest, but wasn't there now—or if he was, he was attempting to cloak his energy so I wouldn't know he was there.

Sadness and loss seemed to permeate my pores as I walked around the large tract of land where the house once stood, and I became overwhelmed by a deep sense of grief and longing. It didn't occur to me until that moment how much I ached to have just a few more minutes in the house. Demon or no demon, I felt that the house and I were inexplicably linked together somehow.

It was with a deep sigh and heavy heart that I reluctantly started to walk back to my truck. As I reached for the door handle, I took one more look back and, in my mind's eye, saw the house still standing there in all its original glory.

Then I felt it, a wave of energy coming at me not unlike the energy I'd felt the night Amon revealed himself to me through the fiery pentagram. I had a quick debate with myself whether to stand my ground or flee. I chose the latter and jerked the door to my Jeep open, jumped in, and raced away from that house as fast I dared.

But I'd found out what I wanted to know—I'd wanted to know if Amon was still nesting there or had moved on to more fertile ground. Not only was he there, he'd regained his strength and was more powerful than ever.

I could only pray that he stayed away from my family and me, although I couldn't have blamed him if he did come after me; after all, I'd gone looking for him.

Second Experience

I had a horrible nightmare. I was in an old house that I didn't recognize with my husband and another person whom I've never seen. We were ghost hunting.

We were looking for a spirit named Annabelle; I don't know anyone named Annabelle either in spirit or living form. I was alone in a room sitting on the floor between a couch and a coffee table.

A breeze started to blow in the room and I called out to my husband to come experience this, but he didn't hear me. Then the breeze turned into a pretty hefty wind. Outside the window I saw bare tree branches swinging in the wind and one of those old-fashioned fly catchers—the kind that are gold and square with holes in them and the sticky strip in the center.

Anyway, I felt something on my back and I called for my husband, but he didn't answer. At first I thought it was the spirit of Annabelle and I told her to get off of me, but she didn't. Then I realized I could be in some serious trouble and crawled over to a large, old, wooden door. On the door was painted a big blue eye in perfect detail. I reached through the semidarkness of the room and got the door opened. As soon as I did that, I was released by the spirit.

Now here's where it gets really weird. I woke up and sat straight up in bed. I looked at the clock on the nightstand and it said 1:58 p.m. Then I heard something else, the sound of a bell, like a church bell. It was right out of that movie *For Whom the Bell Tolls*. It was a single bell and it rang exactly eight times.

I got out of bed to use the bathroom and heard footsteps come out of my bedroom and pass the bathroom door. I thought my husband had gotten out of bed and gone downstairs. Seconds later I went back into the bedroom only to find that my husband was in bed. There's no way he could have made it downstairs and back upstairs in ten seconds.

As soon as I got into bed, my husband got up and went downstairs to use the bathroom and get something to drink. So who walked by the bathroom door? It wasn't one of my dogs; these footsteps sounded like a person walking, not an animal.

I have no idea who Annabelle is or was or what the child spirit was supposed to represent. Dream interpretation dictionaries are of no use to me right now. This is a whole other ball game.

But for the record, an eye like the one I saw could represent the window to my soul, and the bell could represent some kind of warning.

The more I think about the bell, the more it really did sound like a church bell, which could mean salvation. The eye was on the door of the room, and in the dream getting the door open was the only thing that was going to save me. So could the eye have represented a way to save my soul?

Are we back to the whole divine versus evil, light versus dark thing yet again? Is there some unearthly battle going on for my soul? I personally think it would be arrogant to assume that, but right now, with the evidence I have, anything is possible.

And what's up with the tree branches and the fly catcher? The fly catcher I think I can explain: demons lure you into a web, like a spider lures a fly. The tree branches I'm at a loss over.

What really bothers me are the footsteps and the bell. I know I was fully awake. I thought about the bell, footsteps, and the nightmare for the better part of two days and still am not sure exactly what it meant.

My Final Thoughts

Someone once said that hindsight is twenty-twenty, and I think they're right. I have a new outlook on what happened during that time in my life and quite frankly I don't think I'd change a thing.

I'm often asked if given the chance, would I destroy Amon? My answer would have to be no. It goes against everything I believe in.

Writing this book has opened up a lot of old wounds, but has also made me think really hard about all the events that took place since I ran into the Matthews house and the demon Amon, and I've come to some new conclusions—it's amazing what a little time and distance does for the clarity of the mind.

As terrifying as the entire experience with Amon was, in a way, I owe him a debt of gratitude. If I hadn't run into him, I don't think I would be as strong and confident as I am now.

Facing off against Amon taught me a lot about myself. It taught me to be very self-reliant and that when push comes to shove, humans are capable of a lot more than they realize.

I've learned to be fearless in the face of overwhelming odds and other dangerous encounters with the paranormal I've experienced since the events of this book took place.

And, while according to some religions a demon's purpose is to turn you away from God, I found myself becoming closer to God in a way I never thought I would.

While I'm still not a fan of organized religion, my faith and belief in God has been tested by Amon in a way few people will ever experience, and I came out of the events in this book with a much stronger belief in God than I had when I started this adventure.

Throughout the entire experience I always felt as if someone was standing silently by my side, watching over me and helping me, even though I didn't acknowledge it at the time. I feel like I've walked through the fires of hell and came out better for it on the other side.

Truth be told, no one can come in contact with a demon and not come out unscathed or changed in some way. The changes I went through and am still going through have been fundamental. My entire belief system was rocked to the core and was challenged in ways I never thought possible.

However, I feel stronger, confident, and better equipped to handle any situation that is placed before me in ways that wouldn't have been possible had I not encountered Amon.

I wouldn't recommend this method of personal growth to anyone. And, I wouldn't wish what I went through on anyone, not even my worst enemies. It was horrible and terrifying, and it tested me in ways no one should ever have to be tested.

TO WRITE TO THE AUTHOR

If you wish to contact the author or would like more information about this book, please write to the author in care of Llewellyn Worldwide Ltd. and we will forward your request. Both the author and publisher appreciate hearing from you and learning of your enjoyment of this book and how it has helped you. Llewellyn Worldwide Ltd. cannot guarantee that every letter written to the author can be answered, but all will be forwarded. Please write to:

Alexis McQuillan
℅ Llewellyn Worldwide
2143 Wooddale Drive
Woodbury, MN 55125-2989

Please enclose a self-addressed stamped envelope for reply, or $1.00 to cover costs. If outside the U.S.A., enclose an international postal reply coupon.

COLIN WILSON

POLTERGEIST

A Classic Study
in Destructive Haunting

Poltergeist

A Classic Study in Destructive Hauntings

COLIN WILSON

Banging noises and disembodied voices coming from nowhere and everywhere at once. Furniture chasing people through the house. Pots and pans and knives and knick-knacks flying through the air. These are the hallmarks of the poltergeist phenomenon.

In this classic book on destructive hauntings, Colin Wilson, renowned authority on the paranormal, examines the evidence and develops a definitive theory of the poltergeist phenomenon. Countless true-life cases of poltergeist infestations have been recorded since the days of ancient Greece. But what are poltergeists? Where do they come from? And why do they appear in our world? From the case of a huge, black-robed monk that terrorized a family for years, to the investigation of a talking mongoose, to true stories of gnomes, dracu, and demons, this guide explores a fascinating gallery of nasty, noisy entities known as poltergeists.

978-0-7387-1867-5, 384 pp., 6 x 9 $17.95

Marcus F. Griffin
Foreword by Jeff Belanger

EXTREME
PARANORMAL

INVESTIGATIONS

The Blood Farm Horror,
the Legend of Primrose Road,
and Other Disturbing Hauntings

Extreme Paranormal Investigations
The Blood Farm Horror, the Legend of Primrose Road,
and Other Disturbing Hauntings

MARCUS F. GRIFFIN

Foreword by Ghostvillage.com founder and author Jeff Belanger.

Set foot inside the bone-chilling, dangerous, and sometimes downright terrifying world of extreme paranormal investigations. Join Marcus F. Griffin, Wiccan priest and founder of Witches in Search of the Paranormal (WISP), as he and his team explore the Midwest's most haunted properties. These investigations include the creepiest-of-the-creepy cases WISP has tackled over the years, many of them in locations that had never before been investigated. These true-case files include investigations of Okie Pinokie and the Demon Pillar Pigs, the Ghost Children of Munchkinland Cemetery, and the Legend of Primrose Road. Readers will also get an inside glimpse of previously inaccessible places, such as the former Jeffrey Dahmer property as WISP searches for the notorious serial killer's spirit, and the farm that belonged to Belle Gunness, America's first female serial killer and the perpetrator of the Blood Farm Horror.

978-0-7387-2697-7, 264 pp., 5³⁄₁₆ x 8 $15.95